ANGRY BLONDE

BLONDE
EMINEM

ReganBooks
An Imprint of HarperCollinsPublishers

ANGRY BLONDE. Copyright © 2000 by Marshall Mathers III. All rights reserved. Printed in the United States of America. No part of this book may be used or reproduced in any manner whatsoever without written permission except in the case of brief quotations embodied in critical articles and reviews. For information address HarperCollins Publishers Inc., 10 East 53rd Street, New York, NY 10022.

HarperCollins books may be purchased for educational, business, or sales promotional use. For information please write: Special Markets Department, HarperCollins Publishers Inc., 10 East 53rd Street, New York, NY 10022.

FIRST EDITION

Designed by Brent Rollins at ego trip. nyc.
Assistance by Alice Alves

Printed on acid-free paper

Library of Congress Cataloging-in-Publication Data has been applied for.

ISBN 0-06-620922-6

00 01 02 03 04 RRD 10 9 8 7 6 5 4 3 2 1

FOR HAILIE JADE

TABLE OF CONTENTS

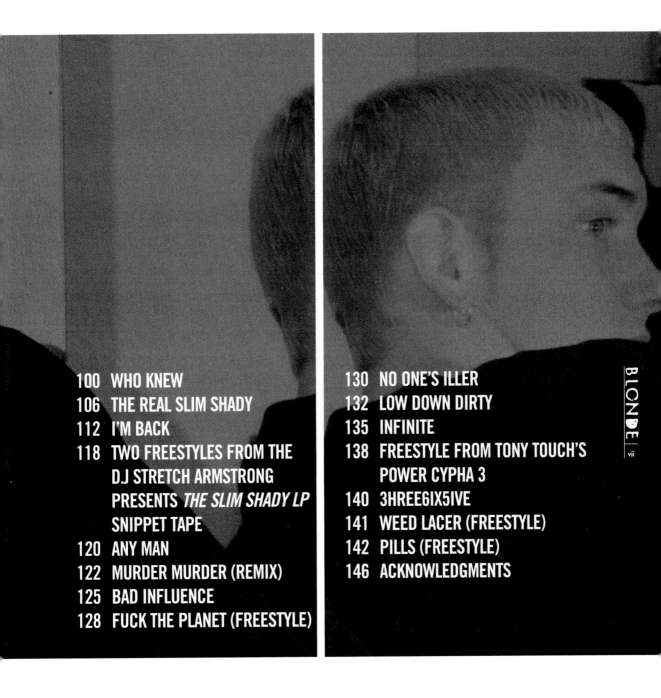

BLONDE vii

The setting was a hotel room in Los Angeles, November 1998. Eminem was in rare form. He'd literally been rhyming all day and was showing no sign of letting up. Words were flowing from his mouth like blood from a stab wound—shocking words, bizarre words, hilarious words. I'm sure the pills and the Bacardi had something to do with it, but his manic energy and twisted humor were forces to behold. Witness the pale presence with a Pentium rhyme processor for a brain: the lifelong rap fan who consumed thousands of songs, logged and sorted them for reference, yet never repeated another rapper's words. He's breaking you down with a brilliantly funny punch line, but he's already composing the next three lines about your boy.

When he wasn't actually rapping—freestyling, free-associating, commenting on people

FOREWORD

around him, all in the form of rhymed verse—he was cracking jokes a mile a minute. A handful of interested parties (friends, label and management reps) stood mute as Eminem carried out a one-man show. No movement, no gesture escaped his eagle eye and sharp tongue. First he would complete your sentence by matching the syllables: "Yo Em, we gotta make sound check" became "No men, we gotta break down necks." Then he'd dis you directly, in your face, to the utter delight of those temporarily escaping his wrath. "Fuck you, you fucking fuck! Your future's fucked, you fuck!" He had fired his friend and loyal manager Paul six or seven times in the last half hour, each time dragging the joke out to excruciating lengths (Paul was apparently used to it). "You're so fat you're fired / You're so fired you're rehired." It was a classic Eminem performance and Marshall Mathers wasn't even a star yet.

This was, actually, a magic moment in Eminem's career: the point just before the Big Bang when his underground buzz reached critical mass and blasted full force into the pop culture mainstream. Em was headlining a show without any official major label product, a relatively rare occurrence in the music business. But enormous fan demand built on the quality of his independent EP and 12-inch vinyl releases was responsible for this performance. *The Slim Shady LP* was finished, the brilliant work with Dr. Dre was in the can, but the music was available only in bootleg form, downloaded and eagerly dubbed by thousands before it was even pressed on vinyl. "My Name Is" had made its way onto the airwaves of a few select rap shows and the response had been overwhelmingly positive. Em was understandably excited and acutely aware of changes in the way people were beginning to perceive him. In anticipation, he shifted his rhyme output to maximum, verbally sparring with imaginary opponents before he stepped into the ring for the main event. It was his final, glorious day in rehearsal for the big show that his life would soon become.

Marshall had shocked even his closest friends a couple of weeks earlier in New York by cropping his hair close and dying it bottle blond. But if he had a master plan, he was keeping it to himself. He took comfort in what he knew best, happily losing himself in intricate rhyme patterns and brilliant, funny turns of phrase. It was becoming increasingly clear that this crazy white kid from the wrong side of the tracks possessed a supreme, undeniable talent. As it turned out, that talent was just the gust of fresh air that pop culture needed.

***

I recently watched a documentary about Quincy Jones in which legend after music legend heaped deserving praise upon the man many consider the greatest producer of all time. In one fascinating moment somebody described Quincy's behavior at the exact

moment when he's inspired to write music. Rare footage showed Q conducting affairs in an early '80s recording session, standing at a podium with a musical score in front of him. Lost in a creative zone, Quincy tilted his head strangely to the side and gestured as if in pain, all the while furiously scribbling. The voice-over continued: "He acts like the notes are stabbing him in the back."

Dr. Dre, rap's greatest producer, displays a Quincy-level mastery of his craft when he provides the musical stage upon which Eminem employs his own curiously personal writing habits. He composes his songs in bits of four or more lines, copied in tiny letters with intentional disregard for the symmetry of the page. As each new sinister couplet comes to him, he shakes his right fist quickly back and forth, in time to a rhythmic pattern known only to him. If everything fits, the message in the words and the flow of the rhyme, he'll chuckle silently to himself and scribble with even more intensity.

The technique seems to be working: Eminem's writing elevates rap to high art yet reaches an enormous, devoted audience. A combination of great ideas, a caustic sense of humor, and an unhealthy dose of morbid self-hate, Em delivers true entertainment value. He's the ultimate scapegoat: no matter how bad a day you're having, his was worse. Many see him as a comedian, and it's true he has a stand-up's flawless timing. But it's his deep mastery of rhythm and language that sets him apart. Each song takes his fans on a ride through his own demented soul, pausing to deride hip-hop, pop culture, and society in general, with just the right dose of catchy hooks and memorable turns of phrase to interest even the most passive ear.

And writing is only half the package; what really sets Marshall apart is his performance ethic. He's a self-admitted "studio rat" who would rather work on new songs than literally do anything else. A perfectionist and vocal virtuoso, he completed "My Name Is" and "Role Model" within an hour of meeting Dr. Dre. Em's active imagination turns records into mini movies featuring multiple characters and cartoonish ad-lib tracks. Recurring figures such as Ken Kaniff, Kim, and now Stan create a Simpsons-like world, occupied by misfits and ruled mercilessly by an unpredictable king.

Like the greats before him—Rakim, KRS-One, LL Cool J, Biggie Smalls, and his hero Tupac— Em combines content and style into a new, exciting genre. His relentless multisyllable rhyme attack pairs words and phrases with an intensity never before heard. As his success exploded into the stratosphere, Eminem remained remarkably down-to-earth, anticipating his critics by dissing himself before they had a chance to.

Oh, and he's certainly white. Can't do anything about it either. As he puts it, "I think I'm gonna try this white thing for a while, see how it works out." Face it, he's the Larry Bird of rap: his race would not be an issue if he weren't so talented. And like Bird, Em will stand forever with the Hall of Famers, respectful of the pioneers but respected in his own right as a creative force who pushes the art form to new heights.

***

Back in L.A., Em finally stumbles to the stage well after midnight, the hours of freestyling and ingesting substances fogging his brain cells. The packed house is alive with people and electricity as their new hero twists his face into a mask of sheer lunacy, spitting furiously into the mike. He puts so much energy into his performance that he eventually slips and falls to his back. It's hilarious and telling: Eminem is exhausted, disoriented, and drunk. But the flow does not stop.

Jonathan Shecter
Founding Editor, **The Source**
President, Game Recordings
New York City
September 2000

ANGRY BLONDE

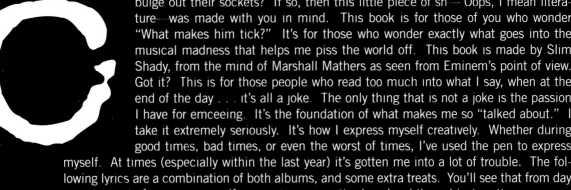

Hi kids. Do you like lyrics? Do you like reading weird shit that'll make your eyes bulge out their sockets? If so, then this little piece of sh — Oops, I mean literature—was made with you in mind. This book is for those of you who wonder "What makes him tick?" It's for those who wonder exactly what goes into the musical madness that helps me piss the world off. This book is made by Slim Shady, from the mind of Marshall Mathers as seen from Eminem's point of view. Got it? This is for those people who read too much into what I say, when at the end of the day . . . it's all a joke. The only thing that is not a joke is the passion I have for emceeing. It's the foundation of what makes me so "talked about." I take it extremely seriously. It's how I express myself creatively. Whether during good times, bad times, or even the worst of times, I've used the pen to express myself. At times (especially within the last year) it's gotten me into a lot of trouble. The following lyrics are a combination of both albums, and some extra treats. You'll see that from day one, my main focus was on self-expression, no matter how lewd the subject matter.

My first album is a combination of everything I went through during my first couple of years as a frustrated emcee. I wanted the public to have this perception of me as a carefree kid who has a lot of problems but tries not to think about them. I wanted people to feel my pain, but to say to them that it's aight. I don't sweat it. Sort of saying that my life was fucked up, but it really didn't bother me. Thing was, the more I started writing and the more I slipped into this Slim Shady character, the more it just started becoming me. My true feelings were coming out, and I just needed an outlet to dump them in. I needed some type of persona. I needed an excuse to let go of all this rage, this dark humor, the pain, and the happiness. Yet I wanted to tell you to take some mushrooms at the end and don't worry about it. Fuck it. But when the album came out I started getting shitted on by critics. A lot of critics thought it was cool, but . . . it was at this point that people started overanalyzing my lyrics.

I remember when Kurt Loder was on the steps of my old house in Detroit doin' the interview and he said, "So when people call you homophobic," and this and that. At first, I didn't understand where he got that impression from. I was shocked 'cause it was the first time I heard it. "Homophobic?" I even asked, "Where did you get that from?" "Well, the original lyrics on 'My Name Is' were 'My Teacher wanted to fuck me in Junior High/ Only problem was my English teacher was a guy.' "

To me there was absolutely nothing homophobic about that line. IT WAS JUST A LINE! It was just something funny, but like most of my lyrics, it got analyzed too much. Right away, people started saying all kinds of shit. Like I don't like gay people. I don't hate gay people, I just don't stray that way. That's not me, I don't care about gay people. Just don't bring that shit around me.

As of late I've had to break it down in layman's terms. Like simply "Let me be me." So for the the sensitive ears out there, let me make "Who Knew," let me make "Stan." And for the people who wanna hear me be me let 'em listen to "Kill You" and "Criminal" and "Marshall Mathers." I feel the current situation has only made me a better emcee. I think as time has passed I've gotten better at what I do. I genuinely learn so much from Dre, because the level of perfection that he works at is amazing. Fuckin' with the best producer in hip-hop music, I had to be more on point. More so than just sittin' around in Detroit and recording songs. When I got in the studio with him, I had to show him something extra . . . I had to be *extra*. The more I learned about music, the more comfortable I felt behind the microphone and the more I could slip into character. It got to a point where I wasn't just worried about getting the rhyme out and sayin' it, I was worried about my pronunciation, about saying shit with authority, or even sometimes saying it softly. That's why I played with the mic a lot more on *The Marshall Mathers* album. I didn't just say my lyrics in one tone, spit the verse and that was it. I learned to play with my voice. I made it do more things that I didn't really know it could do. After *The Slim Shady LP* and Dr. Dre's *Chronic* album, I had simply had more experience behind the mic. I was able to take the whole Slim Shady entity and just run with it on the new album.

After *The Marshall Mathers LP* I upgraded everything. Flow, rhyme character, and the whole shebang. After all these years I feel like I finally made it. Not as a superstar rapper, not as an ill-ass white boy, but as a respected emcee. People are finally aware of the fact that I'm actually saying some shit. Some clever and catchy shit. I may rap about stuff that other rappers don't, but at the end of the day I'm always my own worst critic. I'm always listening to my own shit. When I listen to my songs now, I'll stress myself, thinking, "I could've spit that line better. I should've done that vocal over, I should've done that verse over." Even little things like "I could've popped that '*P*' better on the mic." I listen to songs, thinking "Yeah, it was cool that I came up with that idea to say that, but I didn't execute that rhyme right." There'll always be that one fuckin' word that no one would normally hear, but I hear it. Like *the*. I wonder if I said it "da" or didn't pronounce it right. I'll think, "FUCK! I should've said that shit over." So no matter how ill others might say it is, I always listen to my shit with the mentality that I could have done it better. Until I stop rhyming, I'll always feel like I can do better than I did on the last song that I recorded. And that's the theory, principle, and main rule that I will always live by as an emcee.

ANGRY

STILL DON'T GIVE A FUCK

This was my manager Paul's concept. He called me one day while I was in Cali, saying "You need to do a Just Don't Give a Fuck, Part 2." I responded, "Yeah . . . *still* don't give a fuck." He said, "Just make it have the same feel." He told me this while I was in the middle of writing another song. I forgot what song it was 'cause I was writing like crazy when I got out to Cali. Especially after I got my deal, so I wasn't tryin' to let it slip. I was constantly writing, recording, going back home, and then writing again. "Still Don't Give a Fuck" was one of the songs that I worked on during that massive writing period. The drums on this are the same drums as on "Just Don't Give a Fuck." Only difference was that we added a high hat all through it. Whereas in "Just Don't . . ." the high hat continues so it gives a little more drive to it. To top it off, Jeff from FBT had this ill-ass guitar loop and I thought, "This is it," and then I came up with "I'm zonin' off of one joint / Stoppin' a limo, hopped in the window, shoppin' a demo / at gunpoint." As a matter of fact, the same day we made the beat I once again wrote the song and came with the hook. I wanted this song to sum up the whole album. Basically what the song was sayin' is that no matter what you say about me, or what you think I should do, or what you think of me, of how I should sound or anything . . . I don't give a fuck. This is me. I'ma be it and I'ma stay that way.

A LOT OF PEOPLE ASK ME . . . AM I AFRAID OF DEATH . . .
HELL YEAH I'M AFRAID OF DEATH
I DON'T WANT TO DIE YET
A LOT OF PEOPLE THINK . . . THAT I WORSHIP THE DEVIL . . .
THAT I DO ALL TYPES OF . . . RETARDED SHIT
LOOK, I CAN'T CHANGE THE WAY I THINK
AND I CAN'T CHANGE THE WAY I AM
BUT IF I OFFENDED YOU? GOOD.
'CAUSE I STILL DON'T GIVE A FUCK

I'm zonin' off of one joint, stoppin' a limo
Hopped in the window, shoppin' a demo at gunpoint
A lyricist without a clue, what year is this?
Fuck a needle, here's a sword, bodypierce with this
Livin' amok, never givin' a fuck
Gimme the keys I'm drunk, and I've never driven a truck
But I smoke dope in a cab
I'll stab you with the sharpest knife I can grab
Come back the next week and reopen your scab (YEAH!)
A killer instinct runs in the blood
Emptyin' full clips and buryin' guns in the mud
I've calmed down now—I was heavy once into drugs
I could walk around straight for two months with a buzz
My brain's gone, my soul's worn and my spirit is torn
The rest of my body's still bein' operated on
I'm ducked the fuck down while I'm writin' this rhyme
'Cause I'm probably gonna get struck with lightnin' this time

CHORUS:
FOR ALL THE WEED THAT I'VE SMOKED
—YO THIS BLUNT'S FOR YOU
TO ALL THE PEOPLE I'VE OFFENDED
—YEAH FUCK YOU TOO!
TO ALL THE FRIENDS I USED TO HAVE
—YO I MISS MY PAST
BUT THE REST OF YOU ASSHOLES CAN KISS MY ASS
FOR ALL THE DRUGS THAT I'VE DONE
—YO I'M STILL GON' DO
TO ALL THE PEOPLE I'VE OFFENDED
—YEAH FUCK YOU TOO!
FOR EVERY TIME I REMINISCE
—YO I MISS MY PAST
BUT I STILL DON'T GIVE A FUCK, Y'ALL CAN KISS MY ASS

I walked into a gunfight with a knife to kill you
And cut you so fast when your blood spilled it was still blue
I'll hang you till you dangle and chain you at both ankles
And pull you apart from both angles

I wanna crush your skull till your brains leak out of your veins
And bust open like broken water mains
So tell Saddam not to bother with makin' another bomb
'Cause I'm crushin' the whole world in my palm
Got your girl on my arm and I'm armed with a firearm
So big my entire arm is a giant firebomb
Buy your mom a shirt with a Slim Shady iron-on
And the pants to match ("Here, Momma, try 'em on")
I get imaginative with a mouth full of adjectives, a brain full of adverbs, and a box full of laxatives
Causin' hospital accidents
God help me before I commit some irresponsible acts again

CHORUS

I wanted an album so rugged nobody could touch it
Spent a million a track and went over my budget (Ohh shit!)
Now how in the fuck am I supposed to get out of debt?
I can't rap anymore—I just murdered the alphabet
Drug sickness got me doin' some bugged twitches
I'm withdrawin' from crack so bad my blood itches
I don't rap to get the women—fuck bitches
Give me a fat slut that cooks and does dishes
Never ran with a clique—I'm a posse
Kamikaze, strappin' a motherfuckin' bomb across me
From the second I was born, my momma lost me
I'm a cross between Manson, Esham and Ozzy
I don't know why the fuck I'm here in the first place
My worst day on this earth was my first birthday
Retarded? What did that nurse say? Brain damage?
Fuck, I was born during an earthquake

CHORUS

I'M SHADY

This is a song I wrote in Kim's upstairs apartment. Oh, the memories. I originally wrote this to one of Sade's tracks. I thought of the bass line and we made the song. I already had the rhyme written, so we did the track to the rhyme. Then I kind of fucked with Curtis Mayfield's "Pusherman." It's funny 'cause I didn't get the idea from Mayfield's song. I got it from Ice-T's "Power" record. I didn't know Ice got it from "Pusherman." I used the melody, but I changed the words.

Who came through with two Glocks to terrorize your borough (huh?)
Told you how to slap dips and murder your girl (I did!)
Gave you all the finger and told you to sit and twirl
Sold a billion tapes and still screamed, "Fuck the world!"
(Slim Shady . . .) so come and kill me while my name's hot
And shoot me twenty-five times in the same spot (Ow!)
I think I got a generation brainwashed to pop pills and smoke pot till they brains rot
(uhh-oh)
Stop they blood flow until they veins clot
I need a pain shot, and a shot of plain scotch
Purple haze and acid raindrops
Spike the punch at the party and drank pop (gulp gulp)
Shaved my armpits and wore a tank top

Bad Boy, I told you that I can't stop
You gotta make 'em fear you 'fore you make 'em feel you
So everybody buy my shit or I'ma come and kill you

I GOT MUSHROOMS, I GOT ACID, I GOT TABS AND ASPIRIN TABLETS
I'M YOUR BROTHER WHEN YOU NEED SOME GOOD WEED TO SET YOU FREE
YOU KNOW ME, I'M YOUR FRIEND, WHEN YOU NEED A MINI THIN
(I'M SLIM SHADY . . .) I'M SHADY!!

I like happy things, I'm really calm and peaceful (uh-huh-huh)
I like birds, bees, I like people
I like funny things that make me happy and gleeful (hehehe)
Like when my teacher sucked my wee-wee in preschool (Woo!)
The ill type, I stab myself with a steel spike
While I blow my brain out, just to see what it feels like
'Cause this is how I am in real life (mm-hmm)
I don't want to just die a normal death, I wanna be killed twice (uh-huh)
How you gonna scare somebody with a gun threat
When they high off of drugs they haven't even done yet
(Huh?)
So bring the money by tonight—'cause your wife
Said this the biggest knife she ever saw in her life
(Help me! Help me!)
I try to keep it positive and play it cool
Shoot up the playground and tell the kids to stay in school (Stay in school!)
'Cause I'm the one they can relate to and look up to better
Tonight I think I'll write my biggest fan a fuck you letter

I GOT MUSHROOMS, I GOT ACID, I GOT TABS AND ASPIRIN TABLETS
I'M YOUR BROTHER WHEN YOU NEED SOME GOOD WEED TO SET YOU FREE
YOU KNOW ME, I'M YOUR FRIEND, WHEN YOU NEED A MINI THIN
(I'M SLIM SHADY . . .) I'M SHADY!!

Yo . . . I listen to your demo tape and act like I don't like it
(Aww, that shit is wack!)
Six months later you hear your lyrics on my shit
(What?? That's my shit!)

People don't buy shit no more, they just dub it
That's why I'm still broke and had the number one club hit (yup, uh-huh)
But they love it when you make your business public
So fuck it, I've got herpes while we on the subject (uh-huh)
And if I told you I had AIDS y'all would play it
'Cause you stupid motherfuckers think I'm playin' when I say it
Well, I do take pills, don't do speed

Don't do crack
(uh-uhh)
Don't do coke, I do smoke weed
(uh-uhh)
Don't do smack, I do do 'shrooms, do drink beer
(yup)
I just wanna make a few things clear

My baby mama's not dead (uh-uhh) she's still alive and bitchin' (yup)
And I don't have herpes, my dick's just itchin'
It's not syphilis, and as for being AIDS infested
I don't know yet, I'm too scared to get tested

I GOT MUSHROOMS, I GOT ACID, I GOT TABS AND ASPIRIN TABLETS
I'M YOUR BROTHER WHEN YOU NEED SOME GOOD WEED TO SET YOU FREE
YOU KNOW ME, I'M YOUR FRIEND, WHEN YOU NEED A MINI THIN
(I'M SLIM SHADY . . .) I'M SHADY!!

(Ha hah-ha, ha! Ha hah, hah . . .)
I TOLD YOU I WAS SHADY!!
(Ha hah-ha, hah-ha! Ha hah, hah-ha, hah-ha, hah-ha)
Y'all didn't wanna believe me!
I'M SHADY!!

. . . And that's my name

JUST DON'

"Just Don't Give a Fuck" was a song that I wrote when I was staying at my mother's house. It was also around the time that Hailie was born. She wasn't even a year old yet. All of kinds of shit—not being able to provide for my daughter, my living situation, etc., just started building up so much that I had just had it. "Just Don't Give a Fuck" was actually the second song where people that knew me were like "What the fuck are you talkin' about?" See, I didn't normally talk about stuff like that. It just wasn't my usual subject matter. The very first song I did was called . . . I didn't even have a name for it. It was just two long verses of just rappin' this crazy, ridiculously ill shit. It was so left field from what I was normally doin'. Bizzare, from D-12, was on the ad-libs. I didn't even have a name for it, and at the end he said, "You have now witnessed a white boy on drugs," and it was just talkin' about shit like "Stole your mother's Acura / wrecked it and sold it back to her." It was just a bunch of fucked-up shit. My hype-man, Proof, said, "You need to quit talkin' that drug shit," because it seemed like it was from out of left field compared to what I usually rapped about. I soon found myself doing things that I normally didn't do. Like getting into drugs and drinkin'. I was reeeaaally fucked up. I was sick of everything. Kim and I had Hailie, my producers FBT were just about to give up on me, we weren't payin' rent to my moms, and just a whole bunch of other horrible shit was going on. So "Just Don't Give a Fuck" was the second song that I wrote that was unlike everything else I had done. It was my first real song. It was when I first came up with the whole "Slim Shady" theme. I actually thought of the name and then wrote "Slim Shady / Brain-dead like Jim Brady," and that's when I went with the name.

This song was also on *The Slim Shady EP.*

INTRO: FROGGER
WHOAH!
A GET YOUR HANDS IN THE AIR, AND GET TO CLAPPIN' 'EM AND LIKE, BACK AND FORTH BECAUSE AH
THIS IS . . . WHAT YOU THOUGHT IT WASN'T
IT BEEZ . . . THE BROTHERS REPRESENTIN' THE DIRTY DOZEN
I BE THE F-R-O THE DOUBLE G (COUGHING IN BACKGROUND)
AND CHECK OUT THE MAN HE GOES BY THE NAME OF UH . . .

Slim Shady, brain-dead like Jim Brady
I'm a M80, you Lil' like that Kim lady
I'm buzzin', Dirty Dozen, naughty rotten rhymer
Cursin' at you players worse than Marty Schottenheimer
You wacker than the motherfucker you bit your style from
You ain't gonna sell two copies if you press a double album
Admit it, fuck it, while we comin' out in the open
I'm doin' acid, crack, smack, coke and smokin' dope then
My name is Marshall Mathers, I'm an alcoholic
(Hi Marshall)
I have a disease and they don't know what to call it
Better hide your wallet 'cause I'm comin' up quick to strip your cash
Bought a ticket to your concert just to come and whip your ass
Bitch, I'm comin' out swingin', so fast it'll make your eyes spin
You gettin' knocked the fuck out like Mike Tyson
The +Proof is in the puddin', just ask Deshaun Holton
I'll slit your motherfuckin' throat worse than Ron Goldman

CHORUS:
SO WHEN YOU SEE ME ON YOUR BLOCK WITH TWO GLOCKS
SCREAMIN' "FUCK THE WORLD" LIKE TUPAC
I JUST DON'T GIVE A FUUUUUCK!!
TALKIN' THAT SHIT BEHIND MY BACK, DIRTY MACKIN'
TELLIN' YOUR BOYS THAT I'M ON CRACK
I JUST DON'T GIVE A FUUUUUCK!!
SO PUT MY TAPE BACK ON THE RACK
GO RUN AND TELL YOUR FRIENDS MY SHIT IS WACK
I JUST DON'T GIVE A FUUUUUCK!!
BUT SEE ME ON THE STREET AND DUCK
'CAUSE YOU GON' GET STUCK, STOLE AND SNUFFED
'CAUSE I JUST DON'T GIVE A FUUUUUCK!!

I'm Nicer than Pete, but I'm on a Serch to crush a Miilkbone

I'm Everlast-ing, I melt Vanilla Ice like silicone
I'm ill enough to just straight up dis you for no reason
I'm colder than snow season when it's twenty below freezin'
Flavor with no seasonin', this is the sneak preview
I'll dis your magazine and still won't get a weak review
I'll make your freak leave you, smell the Folgers crystals
This is a lyrical combat, gentlemen, hold your pistols
While I form like Voltron and blast you with my shoulder missiles
Slim Shady, Eminem was the old initials
(Bye-bye!)
Extortion, snortin', supportin' abortion
Pathological liar, blowin' shit out of proportion
The looniest, zaniest, spontaneous, sporadic
Impulsive thinker, compulsive drinker, addict
Half animal, half man
Dumpin' your dead body inside of a fuckin' trash can
With more holes than an afghan

CHORUS

Somebody let me out this limousine (Hey, let me out!)
I'm a caged demon, onstage screamin' like Rage Against the Machine
I'm convinced I'm a fiend, shootin' up while this record is spinnin'
Clinically brain-dead, I don't need a second opinion
Fuck droppin' a jewel, I'm flippin' the sacred treasure
I'll bite your motherfuckin' style, just to make it fresher
I can't take the pressure, I'm sick of bitches
Sick of naggin' bosses bitchin' while I'm washin' dishes
In school I never said much, too busy havin' a head rush
Doin' too much Rush had my face flushed like red blush
Then I went to Jim Beam, that's when my face grayed
Went to gym in eighth grade, raped the women's swim team
Don't take me for a joke, I'm no comedian
Too many mental problems got me snortin' coke and smokin' weed again
I'm goin' up over the curb, drivin' on the median
Finally made it home, but I don't got the key to get in

CHORUS

OUTRO:
Hey, fuck that! Outsidaz . . . Pacewon . . . Young Zee . . .

"Rock Bottom" was (sigh) another song done between the EP and the LP. I didn't know when I wrote it that it was going to come out that sad. I had actually meant it to be an uplifting song, but when we were sitting around making the track, Head had a sample that we played over that beat and it was just so sad. I said fuck it, let's go with this one. Not surprisingly, I wrote it while I was going through a fucked-up time. The night I recorded the song, I had taken a bunch of pills, thrown up, and was just real fucking depressed. So I took a bunch of codeine tablets. Problem was, I took too many of them shits and got real sick. When I wrote the song, it was right before the Rap Olympics happened. It was during the week when I had gotten evicted from my house. I was stayin' across the street from where

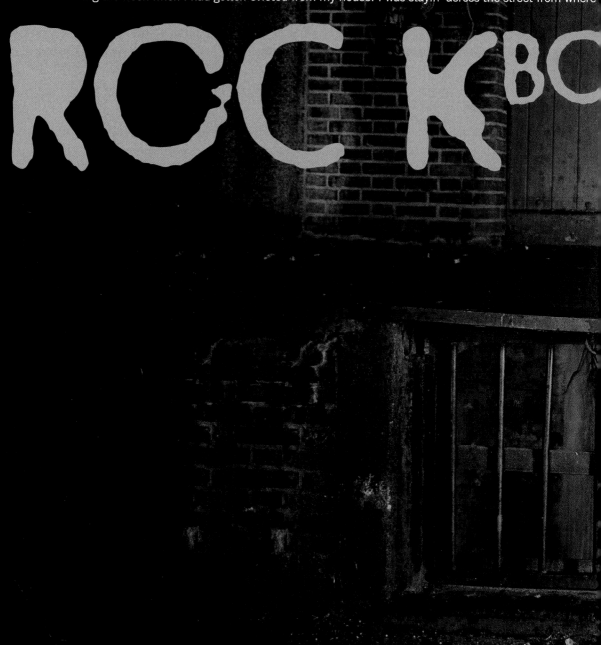

ANGRY

ROCKBO

I used to live. It was a street called Novara out in Detroit. I was staying with these two roommates, and this dude told me that he had cheaper rent for me and that I should come live with him. We said "Okay he's got cheaper rent, then fuck it, we'll move in his house." So me and my boy went across the street to live with him. We were paying our rent to him, but the s.o.b. was keeping our rent and wasn't payin' the landlord. He took the rent, saved up his own money, and bounced on us. So one day we come home and all our shit's on the fuckin' front lawn. We never could catch that motherfucker. Till this day, we haven't caught him. It was a real fucked period in my life (no surprise there), and I felt like I had hit "rock bottom."

TTCM

BLONDE 010

AH YEAH, YO!
THIS SONG IS DEDICATED TO ALL THE HAPPY PEOPLE
ALL THE HAPPY PEOPLE WHO HAVE REAL NICE LIVES
AND WHO HAVE NO IDEA WHAT'S IT LIKE TO BE BROKE AS FUCK

VERSE ONE:
I feel like I'm walking a tight rope, without a circus net
Popping Percocets, I'm a nervous wreck
I deserve respect; but I work a sweat for this worthless check
'Bout to burst this tech, at somebody to reverse this debt
Minimum wage got my adrenaline caged

Full of venom and rage
Especially when I'm engaged
And my daughter's down to her last diaper
That's got my ass hyper
I pray that God answers, maybe I'll ask nicer
Watching ballers while they flossing in their Pathfinders
These overnight stars becoming autograph signers
We all long to blow up and leave the past behind us
Along with the small fries and average half-pinters
While playa haters turn bitch like they have vaginas
'Cause we see them dollar signs and let the cash blind us
Money will brainwash you and leave your ass mindless
Snakes slither in the grass spineless

CHORUS (REPEAT 2X):
THAT'S ROCK BOTTOM
WHEN THIS LIFE MAKES YOU MAD ENOUGH TO KILL
THAT'S ROCK BOTTOM
WHEN YOU WANT SOMETHING BAD ENOUGH TO STEAL
THAT'S ROCK BOTTOM
WHEN YOU FEEL YOU HAVE HAD IT UP TO HERE
'CAUSE YOU MAD ENOUGH TO SCREAM BUT YOU SAD ENOUGH TO TEAR

VERSE TWO:
My life is full of empty promises
And broken dreams
Hopin' things look up
But there ain't no job openings
I feel discouraged, hungry, and malnourished
Living in this house with no furnace, unfurnished
And I'm sick of working dead-end jobs with lame pay
And I'm tired of being hired and fired the same day
But fuck it, if you know the rules to the game—play
'Cause when we die we know we're all going the same way
It's cool to be the player, but it sucks to be the fan

When all you need is bucks to be the man
Plush luxury sedan
Or comfortable and roomy in a six but
They threw me in the mix
With all these gloomy lunatics
Who walk around depressed
And smoke a pound of cess a day

And yesterday went by so quick it seems like it was just today
My daughter wants to throw the ball but I'm too stressed to play
Live half my life and throw the rest away

CHORUS

There's people that love me and people that hate me
But it's the evil that made me this backstabbing, deceitful, and shady
I want the money, the women, the fortune, and the fame
If it means I'll end up burning in hell scorching in flames
If it means I'm stealing your checkbook and forging your name
It's lifetime bliss for eternal torture and pain
'Cuz right now I feel like I just hit the rock bottom
I got problems now everybody on my block's got 'em
I'm screaming like those two cops when 2Pac shot 'em
Holding two Glocks, I hope your door's got new locks on 'em
My daughter's feet ain't got no shoes or socks on 'em
And them rings you wearing look like they got a few rocks on 'em
And while you flaunt 'em I could be taking them to shops to pawn 'em
I got a couple of rings and a brand-new watch, you want 'em?
'Cuz I ain't never went gold off of one song
I'm running up on someone's lawn with guns drawn

CHORUS

M0415 | MEZZ1 G

EVENT CODE | SECTION/BOX

$ 0.00 | GENADM/SE

PRICE & ALL TAXES INCL.

METROPO

CONVENIENCE CHARGE | E

MEZZ1

SECTION/BOX | 311 WES

0 7X

A1 314 | HAMMER

ROW   SEAT

BR601C | AT THE N

5APR99 | THU APR

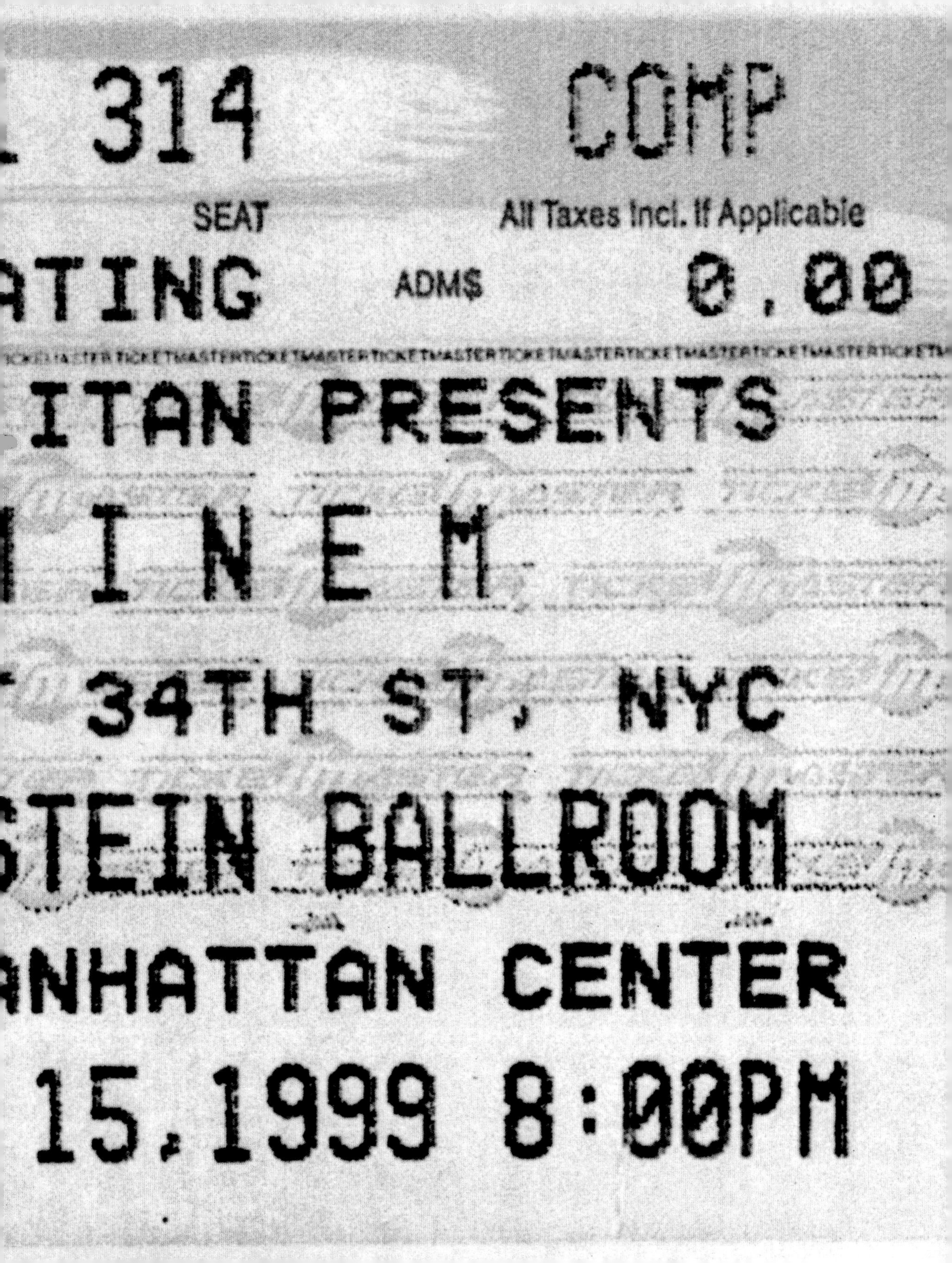

314
COMP
SEAT
All Taxes Incl. If Applicable
ATING
ADM$
0.00
TICKETMASTERTICKETMASTERTICKETMASTERTICKETMASTER
ITAN PRESENTS
INEM
34TH ST, NYC
STEIN BALLROOM
ANHATTAN CENTER
15,1999 8:00PM

"Cum On Everybody" was another song I did between the EP and the LP. I wanted to make a dance parody. It was during that Puffy stage, when Puff was really hot. So when I wrote the song, I thought, "What if I made a dance song my way?" So I was taking the most ridiculous shit and then coming in with the hook, "Cum on every-

CUM ON EVERY

[GIRL]
HMM-HMM-HMHMHMMHM . . . AHHH, WHOOOOO!! SHIT
[EMINEM]
YO, MIC CHECK
TESTING ONE, TWO, UM . . . TWELVE
(whattup whattup whattup . . . Outsidaz)
[EMINEM]
THIS IS MY DANCE SONG
(Outsidaz)
CAN YOU HEAR ME?
(Rah Digga, Pacewon, Young Zee)
[EMINEM]
AIGHT, AY TURN MY HEADPHONES UP
(bust it bust it)

body." Head did the original beat to it. I already had the hook, the hook was easy: "Cum on every-body get down tonight / If you ever see a video for this shit / I'd probably be dressed up like a mummy with my wrist slit / Cum on everybody." No matter what I was talking about in the song, the subject would quickly change into some party shit.

BCDY

My favorite color is red, like the bloodshed
From Kurt Cobain's head, when he shot him-
self dead
Women all grabbin' at my shishkebob
Bought Lauryn Hill's tape so her kids could starve
(I can't stand white people!)
You thought I was ill, now I'm even more so
Shit, I got full-blown AIDS and a sore throat
I got a wardrobe with an orange robe (wolf whistle)
I'm in the fourth row, signin' autographs at your show
(Yo, can you sign this right here?)
I just remembered that I'm absentminded
Wait, I mean I've lost my mind, I can't find it
I'm freestylin' every verse that I spit
'Cause I don't even remember the words to my shit
(umm, one two)
I told the doc I need a change in sickness
And gave a girl herpes in exchange for syphilis
Put my LP on your Christmas gift list
You wanna get high, here, bitch, just sniff this

CUM ON EVERYBODY—GET DOWN TONIGHT (8X)

Yo . . . yo yo yo yo
I tried suicide once and I'll try it again
That's why I write songs where I die at the end
'Cause I don't give a fuck, like my middle finger
was stuck
And I was wavin' it at everybody screamin', "I suck"
(I SUCK!!!)
I'll go onstage in front of a sellout crowd
And yell out loud, "All y'all get the hell out now"
Fuck rap, I'm givin' it up y'all, I'm sorry
(But Eminem this is your record release party!)

I'm bored out of my gourd—so I took a hammer
And nailed my foot to the floorboard of my Ford
Guess I'm just a sick sick bastard
Who's one sandwich short of a picnic basket (I ain't
got it all)
One Excedrin tablet short of a full medicine cabinet
I feel like my head has been shredded like lettuce
and cabbage
(ohhhhhhh) And if you ever see a video for this shit
I'll probably be dressed up like a mummy with my
wrists slit

CUM ON EVERYBODY—GET DOWN TONIGHT (8X)

Got bitches on my jock out in East Detroit
'Cause they think that I'm a motherfuckin' Beastie
Boy (wolf whistle)
So I told 'em I was Mike D
They was like, "Gee I don't know, he might be!"
I told 'em,

"Meet me at Kid Rock's next concert
I'll be standin' by the Loch Ness Monster (okay)
peace out (bye!!)"
Then I jetted to the weed house
Smoked out, till I started bustin' freestyles
Broke out, then I dipped quick back to the crib, put
on lipstick
Crushed up the Tylenol and ate it with a dipstick
(slurping)
Made a couple of crank calls collect
(brrrrrrrring, click)
"It's Ken Kaniff from Connecticut, can you accept?"
I wanna make songs all the fellas love
And murder every rich rapper that I'm jealous of
So just remember when I bomb your set

Yo, I only cuss to make your mom upset

CUM ON EVERYBODY—GET DOWN TONIGHT (20X)

MY FAULT

The "Lounge" skit that goes before "My Fault" actually inspired the mushroom song. Jeff from FBT and I were in the studio and we had just knocked out a song, but we were trying to come up with more shit. Jeff was just sitting there, fuckin' around, singing a song that went something like "I never meant to . . ." Now, he never said, "give you mushrooms." I finished it off and we both just started singin' it. We were laughin' and jokin' around and shit, until he went into this faster, more up-tempo rendition. He started singing, "I never meant to give you mushrooms, girl, I never . . ." And I just finished the hook off. It was really late at night, so we just came back and knocked it out the next day. We made the track first and then I took it home and wrote to it.

"My Fault" is actually sort of a story about one of my friends who had a bad acid trip. But it was a dude, though. He was having a bad trip and was talkin' about how he was worthless, how he didn't have a job, and how he was just fucked up. He was going through a depressed stage and was even crying. I told him, "Yo, it's okay." So I thought, "What if I wrote it about a girl who's fucked up having a bad mushroom trip?" It was actually going to be a single. I had done a clean version of it, and put it on the *Celebrity Death Match* soundtrack. Interscope didn't want to release it as a single, though, 'cause if I came with that after "My Name Is" instead of "Guilty Conscience," I would've looked like a fuckin' bubblegum artist. Two goofy songs right back-to-back. That probably would've fucked me up till this day. The song . . . not the 'shrooms.

Eminem does the voices of all characters in the song

CHORUS (REPEAT 2X):
I NEVER MEANT TO GIVE YOU MUSHROOMS, GIRL
I NEVER MEANT TO BRING YOU TO MY WORLD
NOW YOU SITTING IN THE CORNER CRYING
AND NOW IT'S MY FAULT, MY FAULT

[EMINEM]

I went to John's rave with Ron and Dave
And met a new wave blonde babe with half of her head shaved
A nurse's aide who came to get laid and tied up
With first-aid tape and raped on the first date
Susan—an ex-heroin addict who just stopped usin'
Who love booze and alternative music
(Whattup?)
Told me she was goin' back into usin' again
(Nah!)
I said, "Wait, first try this hallucinogen
It's better than heroin, Henn, the booze, or the gin
C'mere, let's go in here"

[knocks on the door]

"Who's in the den?"
[RON]
"It's me and Kelly!"
"My bad, (sorry) let's try another room"
[SUSAN]
I don't trust you!
"Shut up slut!
Chew up this mushroom
This'll help you get in touch with your roots
We'll get barefoot, butt naked, and run in the woods"
[SUSAN]
Oh hell, I might as well try 'em, this party is so drab
"Oh dag!!"
[SUSAN]
What?
"I ain't mean for you to eat the whole bag!"
[SUSAN]
Huh?!

CHORUS

"Yo Sue!"

[SUSAN]

Get away from me, I don't know you

Oh shoot, she's tripping . . .

[SUSAN]

I need to go puke!!

(Bleahh!)

I wasn't tryin' to turn this into somethin' major

I just wanted to make you appreciate nature

Susan, stop cryin', I don't hate ya

The world's not against you, I'm sorry your father raped you

So what you had your little coochie in your dad's mouth?

That ain't no reason to start wiggin' and spaz out

She said,

[SUSAN]

Help me I think I'm havin' a seizure!

I said, "I'm high too, bitch, quit grabbin' my T-shirt (Let go!)

Would you calm down, you're startin' to scare me"

She said,

[SUSAN]

I'm twenty-six years old and I'm not married

I don't even have any kids and I can't cook

(Hello!)

"I'm over here, Sue, (hi) you're talkin' to the plant, look!

We need to get to a hospital 'fore it's too late

'Cause I never seen no one eat as many 'shrooms as you ate

CHORUS

"Susan (wait!) Where you goin'? You better be careful"

[SUSAN]

Leave me alone, Dad, I'm sick of gettin' my hair pulled

"I'm not your dad, quit tryin' to swallow your tongue

Want some gum? Put down the scissors, 'fore you do somethin' dumb

I'll be right back, just chill, baby, please?

I gotta go find Dave, he's the one who gave me these

John, where's Dave at before I bash you?"

[JOHN]

He's in the bathroom; I think he's takin' a crap, dude!

"Dave! Pull up your pants,

we need an ambulance

There's a girl upstairs talkin' to plants

Choppin' her hair off, and there's only two days left
To spring break, how long do these things take to wear off?"

[DAVE]

Well, it depends on how many you had

"I took three, she ate the other twenty-two caps
Now she's upstairs cryin' out her eyeballs, drinkin' Lysol"

[DAVE]

She's gonna die, dude

"I know and it's my fault!"

[DAVE]

My god!!!

CHORUS

MY GOD, I'M SO SORRY!
I'M SO SORRY!
SUSAN PLEASE WAKE UP!
PLEASE! PLEASE WAKE UP!!
WHAT ARE YOU DOING?!
YOU'RE NOT DEAD!! YOU'RE NOT DEAD!
I KNOW YOU'RE NOT DEAD! OH MY GOD!

SUSAN, WAKE UP! OH GOD . . .

'97
BONNIE
AND
CLYDE

This little "topic of discussion" was also written in the summer of '97. Again, during that time a lot of fucked-up shit just started snowballin' for me. It was also when Kim and I weren't really seeing eye to eye and whatnot. See, we weren't together and she was using my daughter, Hailie, as a weapon against me and she wasn't lettin' me see her. I originally wrote the song to get back at her so that she could hear it. I didn't write the song thinking that I was gonna get a fuckin' record deal and that this was a song that was going to be huge, or even talked about. I mean, at the most I thought it would be talked about in Detroit, but I didn't figure I was going to get a deal and go nationwide with it. My original reason for making it was to piss her off. I even went so far as to use Hailie for the vocal you hear on the record. It was my little baby's first musical appearance. Regardless, I think it's one of my favorite concept songs. Originally, DJ Head made the beat. It didn't sound like the Bill Withers version anymore. Head had the bass line going down like "tunt-tu-tunt tunt tad dunt, tunt-tu-tunt tunt tad dunt." So it just clicked in my head instantly. A song about just me and my daughter. The timing was perfect on it. I got the beat, thought of the hook and what to write about. But I thought, "How can I make a song about Hailie?" I didn't want to make the shit corny or nothing, but I was also tryin' to piss Kim off. I put a lot of my personal shit out there. But I don't care. See, it's like every time somebody disses me, I'ma talk about them. It's kind of like if you piss me off, I'ma respond in my songs. Okay, Kim, you're going to piss me off? Then I'ma make you look stupid in front of all these people. But I don't limit this attitude to just Kim . . . I mean anybody.

JUST THE TWO OF US . . . (8X)

Baby, your da-da loves you
(hey)
And I'ma always be here for you
(hey)
no matter what happens
You're all I got in this world, I would never give you
up for nothin'
Nobody in this world is ever gonna keep you from me
I love you

C'mon, Hai-Hai, we goin' to the beach
Grab a couple of toys and let Da-da strap you in the
car seat
Oh where's Mama? She's takin' a little nap in the trunk

Oh that smell
(whew!)
Da-da musta runned over a skunk
Now I know what you're thinkin'—it's kind of late to
go swimmin'
But you know your mama, she's one of those
type of women
That do crazy things, and if she don't get her way,
she'll throw a fit
Don't play with Da-da's toy knife, honey, let go of it
(no!)
And don't look so upset, why you actin' bashful?
Don't you wanna help Da-da build a sand castle?
(yeah!)
And Mama said she wants to show how far she can float
And don't worry about that little boo-boo on

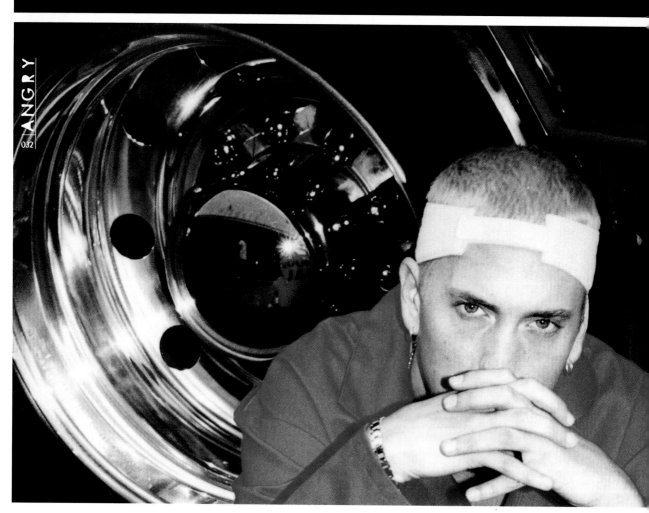

her throat

It's just a little scratch—it don't hurt, her was eatin' dinner

While you were sweepin' and spilled ketchup on her shirt

Mama's messy, ain't she? We'll let her wash off in the water

And me and you can pway by ourselves, can't we?

> JUST THE TWO OF US . . . (2X)
> AND WHEN WE RIDE!
> JUST THE TWO OF US . . . (2X)
> JUST YOU AND I!
> JUST THE TWO OF US . . . (2X)
> AND WHEN WE RIDE!
> JUST THE TWO OF US . . . (2X)
> JUST YOU AND I!

See, honey . . . there's a place called heaven and a place called hell

A place called prison and a place called jail

And Da-da's probably on his way to all of 'em except one

'Cause Mama's got a new husband and a stepson

And you don't want a brother do ya?

(Nah)

Maybe when you're old enough to understand a little better

I'll explain it to ya

But for now we'll just say Mama was real real bad

She was bein' mean to Dad and made him real real mad

But I still feel sad that I put her on time-out

Sit back in your chair, honey, quit tryin' to climb out

(WAHH!)
I told you it's okay, Hai-Hai, wanna ba-ba?
Take a night-night? Nan-a-boo, goo-goo ga-ga?
Her make goo-goo ca-ca? Da-da change your dia-dee
Clean the baby up so her can take a nighty-nighty
And Dad'll wake her up as soon as we get to the water
Ninety-seven Bonnie and Clyde, me and my daughter

    JUST THE TWO OF US . . . (2X)
    AND WHEN WE RIDE!
    JUST THE TWO OF US . . . (2X)
    JUST YOU AND I!
    JUST THE TWO OF US . . . (2X)
    AND WHEN WE RIDE!
    JUST THE TWO OF US . . . (2X)
    JUST YOU AND I!

Wake up sweepy head we're here, before we pway
We're gonna take Mama for a wittle walk along the pier
Baby, don't cry, honey, don't get the wrong idea
Mama's too sweepy to hear you screamin' in her ear
(Ma-maa!)
That's why you can't get her to wake, but don't worry
Da-da made a nice bed for Mommy at the bottom of
the lake
Here, you wanna help Da-da tie a rope around this
rock? (yeah!)
We'll tie it to her footsie, then we'll roll her off the dock
Ready now, here we go, on the count of free . . . One
. . . two . . . free . . . WHEEEEEE!
(Whooooooshhhhh)
There goes Mama, spwashin' in the water

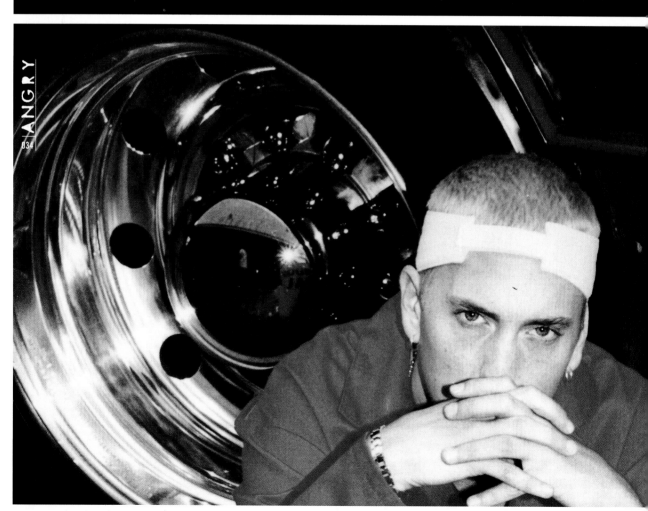

ANGRY

034

No more fightin' wit Dad, no more restraining order
No more Step-da-da, no more new brother
Blow her kisses bye-bye, tell Mama you love her
(Mommy!)
Now we'll go play in the sand, build a castle and junk
But first, just help Dad with two more things out
the trunk

JUST THE TWO OF US . . . (2X)
AND WHEN WE RIDE!
JUST THE TWO OF US . . . (2X)
JUST YOU AND I!
JUST THE TWO OF US . . . (2X)
AND WHEN WE RIDE!
JUST THE TWO OF US . . . (2X)
JUST YOU AND I!

JUST THE TWO OF US . . . (4X)

Just me and you baby is all we need in this world
Just me and you
Your da-da will always be there for you
Your da-da's always gonna love you
Remember that
If you ever need me I will always be here for you
If you ever need anything,
just ASK
Da-da will be right there
Your da-da loves you
I love you, baby

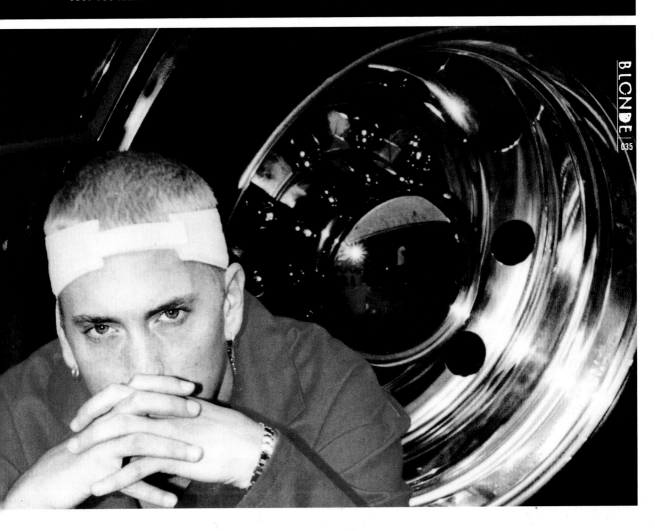

BLONDE
035

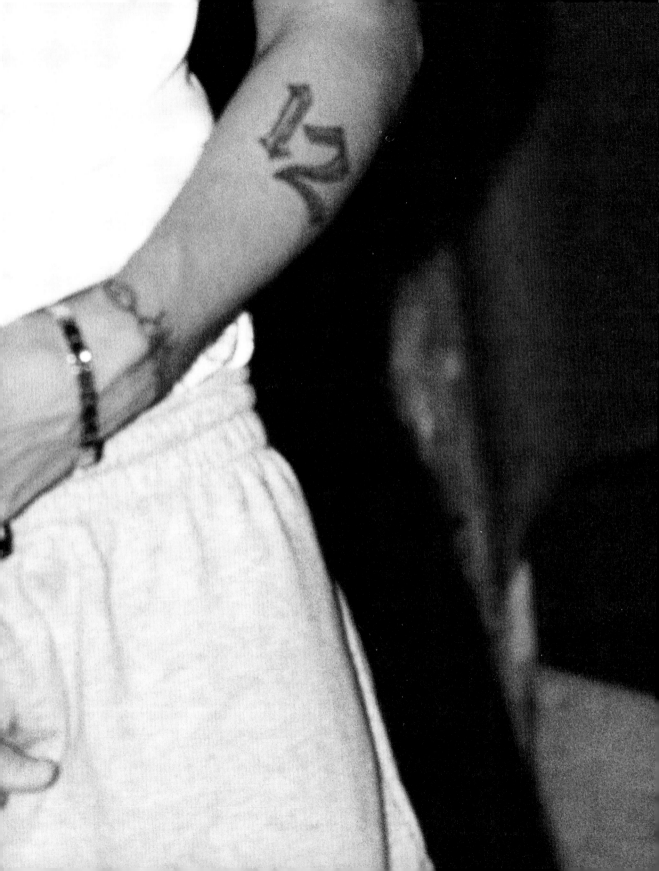

IF I HAD

"If I Had" was off *The Slim Shady EP*. It was written when I was stayin' at a friend's house. I was living with a couple of roommates at the time. I wrote that shit the same week my car broke down. My fuckin' engine blew out and a bunch of fucked-up shit was happening all at the same time. I wrote the song during the summer of '97, but I didn't record it until that winter. That's when I recorded the whole EP in about two weeks. Interscope heard it, liked it, and wanted to use it for the LP.

Life . . . by Marshall Mathers
What is life?
Life is like a big obstacle
Put in front of your optical to slow you down
And every time you think you gotten past it
It's gonna come back around and tackle you to
the damn ground
What are friends?
Friends are people that you think are your friends
But they really your enemies, with secret identities
And disguises, to hide they true colors
So just when you think you close enough to be
brothers
They wanna come back and cut your throat when
you ain't lookin'
What is money?
Money is what makes a man act funny
Money is the root of all evil
Money'll make them same friends come back
around
Swearing that they was always down
What is life?
I'm tired of life

I'm tired of backstabbing ass snakes with
friendly grins
I'm tired of committing so many sins
Tired of always giving in when this bottle of
Henny wins
Tired of never having any ends
Tired of having skinny friends hooked on crack
and Mini Thins
I'm tired of this DJ playing YOUR shit when he spins
Tired of not having a deal
Tired of having to deal with the bullshit without
grabbing the steel
Tired of drowning in my sorrow
Tired of having to borrow a dollar for gas to start
my Monte Carlo
I'm tired of motherfuckers sprayin' shit and
dartin' off
I'm tired of jobs startin' off at five-fifty an hour
Then this boss wonders why I'm smartin' off
I'm tired of being fired every time I fart and cough
Tired of having to work as a gas station clerk
For this jerk breathing down my neck driving
me berserk
I'm tired of using plastic silverware
Tired of working in Building Square
Tired of not being a millionaire

BLONDE

CHORUS:
BUT IF I HAD A MILLION DOLLARS
I'D BUY A DAMN BREWERY, AND TURN THE
PLANET INTO ALCOHOLICS
IF I HAD A MAGIC WAND, I'D MAKE THE WORLD
SUCK MY DICK
WITHOUT A CONDOM ON, WHILE I'M ON THE JOHN
IF I HAD A MILLION BUCKS
IT WOULDN'T BE ENOUGH, BECAUSE I'D STILL BE
OUT ROBBING ARMORED TRUCKS
IF I HAD ONE WISH
I WOULD ASK FOR A BIG ENOUGH ASS FOR THE
WHOLE WORLD TO KISS

I'm tired of being white trash, broke and always poor
Tired of taking pop bottles back to the party store
I'm tired of not having a phone
Tired of not having a home to have one in if I did
have it on
Tired of not driving a BM
Tired of not working at GM, tired of wanting to be him
Tired of not sleeping without a Tylenol PM
Tired of not performing in a packed coliseum
Tired of not being on tour
Tired of fucking the same blond whore after work
In the back of a Contour
I'm tired of faking knots with a stack of ones
Having a lack of funds and resorting back to guns
Tired of being stared at
I'm tired of wearing the same damn Nike Air hat
Tired of stepping in clubs wearing the same pair
of Lugz
Tired of people saying they're tired of hearing me
rap about drugs
Tired of other rappers who ain't bringin' half the

skill as me
Saying they wasn't feeling me on "Nobody's As Ill
As Me"
I'm tired of radio stations telling fibs
Tired of JLB saying "Where Hip-Hop Lives"

BUT IF I HAD A MILLION DOLLARS
I'D BUY A DAMN BREWERY, AND TURN THE
PLANET INTO ALCOHOLICS
IF I HAD A MAGIC WAND, I'D MAKE THE WORLD
SUCK MY DICK
WITHOUT A CONDOM ON, WHILE I'M ON THE JOHN
IF I HAD A MILLION BUCKS
IT WOULDN'T BE ENOUGH, BECAUSE I'D STILL BE
OUT ROBBING ARMORED TRUCKS
IF I HAD ONE WISH
I WOULD ASK FOR A BIG ENOUGH ASS FOR THE
WHOLE WORLD TO KISS

You know what I'm sayin'?
I'm tired of all of this bullshit
Telling me to be positive
How'm I s'posed to be positive when I don't see
shit positive?
Know what I'm sayin'?
I rap about shit around me, shit I see
Know what I'm sayin'?
Right now I'm tired of everything
Tired of all this player hating that's going on in
my own city
Can't get no airplay, you know what I'm sayin'?
But hey, it's cool though, you know what I'm sayin'?
Just fed up
That's my word

BRAIN DAMAGE

'Brain Damage" was actually a song that I wrote in between *The Slim Shady EP* and the LP. wrote it while I was chillin' in this little duplex that Kim was stayin' in right before went to Cali. I wrote the first verse there and wrote the hook, but I was going to thro the song out. I started throwing a lot of my songs away when we didn't get a recor deal. Then, when we got the deal, I was going over the first verse and the hook lik 'This shit is crazy. You know what? Let me finish this." I finished the second verse out in Cali i he little apartment the label put me up in when I got my deal. I originally wrote it to a scrap bea Jntil a few days later, when I just started thinkin' of the bass line in my head and the way that should go. Then we did the version you hear on the album. It's only two verses, one of regula ength and the other a fuckin' long-ass verse.

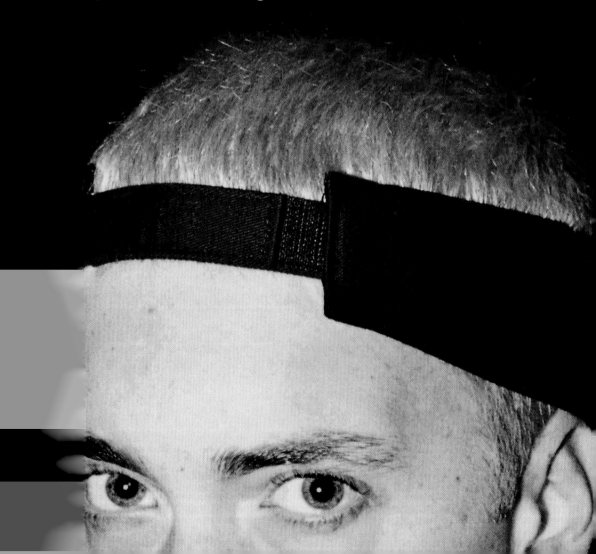

[DOCTOR]
  Scalpel
[NURSE]
  Here
[DOCTOR]
  Sponge
[NURSE]
  Here
[DOCTOR]
  Wait . . . he's convulsing, he's convulsing!
[NURSE]
  Ah!
[DOCTOR]
  We're gonna have to shock him!
[NURSE]
  Oh my! Oh my God!
[DOCTOR]
  We're gonna have to shock him!
[NURSE]
  Oh my God!

These are the results of a thousand electric volts
A neck with bolts, "Nurse, we're losin' him, check the pulse!"
A kid who refused to respect adults
Wore spectacles with taped frames and a freckled nose
A corny-lookin' white boy, scrawny and always ornery
'Cause I was always sick of brawny bullies pickin' on me
And I might snap, one day just like that
I decided to strike back and flatten every tire on the bike rack (Whosssssh)
My first day in junior high, this kid said, "It's you and I, three o'clock sharp this afternoon you die"
I looked at my watch, it was one-twenty
"I already gave you my lunch money, what more do you want from me?!?"
He said, "Don't try to run from me, you'll just make it worse . . ." My palms were sweaty, and I started to shake at first
Something told me, "Try to fake a stomachache—it works"
I screamed, "Owww! My appendix feels like they could burst!
Teacher, teacher, quick I need a naked nurse!"
[NURSE]
"What's the matter?"
[EMINEM]
"I don't know, my leg, it hurts!"

[NURSE]
"Leg?!? I thought you said it was your tummy?!?"
[EMINEM]
"Oh, I mean it is, but I also got a bum knee!"
[NURSE]
"Mr. Mathers, the fun and games are over.
And just for that stunt, you're gonna get some extra homework."
[EMINEM]
"But don't you wanna give me after-school detention?"
[NURSE]
"Nah, that bully wants to beat your ass and I'ma let him."

CHORUS (REPEAT 2X) :
BRAIN DAMAGE, EVER SINCE THE DAY I WAS BORN
DRUGS IS WHAT THEY USED TO SAY I WAS ON
THEY SAY I NEVER KNEW WHICH WAY I WAS GOIN'
BUT EVERYWHERE I GO THEY KEEP PLAYIN' MY SONG

Brain damage . . . Way before my baby daughter Hailie
I was harassed daily by this fat kid named D'Angelo Bailey
An eighth-grader who acted obnoxious, 'cause his father boxes
So every day he'd shove me in the lockers
One day he came in the bathroom while I was pissin'
And had me in the position to beat me into submission
He banged my head against the urinal till he broke my nose
Soaked my clothes in blood, grabbed me and choked my throat
I tried to plead and tell him, "We shouldn't beef"
But he just wouldn't leave, he kept chokin' me and I couldn't breathe
He looked at me and said, "You gonna die honkey!"
The principal walked in (What's going on in here?)
And started helpin' him stomp me
I made them think they beat me to death
Holdin' my breath for like five minutes before they finally left
Then I got up and ran to the janitor's storage booth

Kicked the door hinge loose and ripped out the four-inch screws
Grabbed some sharp objects, brooms, and foreign tools
"This is for every time you took my orange juice,
Or stole my seat in the lunchroom and drank my chocolate milk.
Every time you tipped my tray and it dropped and spilt.
I'm getting you back bully! Now once and for good."
I cocked the broomstick back and swung hard as I could
And beat him over the head with it till I broke the wood
Knocked him down, stood on his chest with one foot . . .
. . . Made it home, later that same day
Started readin' a comic, and suddenly everything became gray
I couldn't even see what I was tryin' to read
I went deaf, and my left ear started to bleed
My mother started screamin', "What are you on, drugs?!?
Look at you, you're gettin' blood all over my rug!" (Sorry!)
She beat me over the head with the remote control
Opened a hole, and my whole brain fell out of my skull
I picked it up and screamed, "Look, bitch, what have you done?!?"
[MOTHER]
"Oh my God, I'm sorry, son"
[EMINEM]
"Shut up, you cunt!" I said. "Fuck it!"
Took it and stuck it back up in my head
Then I sewed it shut and put a couple of screws in my neck

CHORUS

BRAIN DAMAGE . . .
IT'S BRAIN DAMAGE . . .
I GOT BRAIN DAMAGE . . .
IT'S BRAIN DAMAGE . . .
IT'S PROBABLY BRAIN DAMAGE . . .
IT'S BRAIN DAMAGE . . .
BRAIN DAMAGE . . .
I GOT BRAIN DAMAGE . . .

ROLE MODEL

I was just fuckin' around when I made this song. To me it's just a rap record. The message behind it was just complete sarcasm. I wanted to be clear: Don't look at me like I'm a fucking role model. Dre and I were in the studio at his house, and he had made the track first. I had started a rhyme the night before and I hadn't finished it yet. When I heard the track, I said, "Yo Dre, I got a rhyme that goes with that." I finished the rhyme and started writing the song in the studio. I finished the first verse, knocked out the second verse, and then wrote a hook. Then Mel-Man thought of the part that goes "Don't you wanna grow up to be just like me?" I said, "Yo, that's perfect," 'cause I was talkin' about the same shit. You know, smoke weed, take pills, drop out of school, and all that shit. So he had that part of the hook and I filled in all the blanks. "I came to the club drunk with a fake ID / Don't you wanna grow up to be just like me!" This was one of the first three songs I did with Dre when we began working together.

Shady Note: The other two songs I did with Dre in the first studio session never got used for any-thing. One was a song called "When Hell Freezes Over." It was actually the first dis I did against Insane Clown Posse. The other joint I did with Dre was called "Ghost Stories." It was a song I was gonna do with an emcee colleague of mine, Thirstin' Howl III. I had a verse, Dre had a track, and he asked, "Are you diggin' this?" I said, "Yeah, I got a rhyme to spit to it," but it was only one long verse. It was a story about being trapped in a haunted house and the walls were bleeding and all kinds of crazy shit. Like some poltergeist type shit, but it never got used for anything. So neither one of us got to use it for nothin'. Oh well, maybe next album.

Okay, I'm going to attempt to drown myself
You can try this at home
You can be just like me!

Mic check one, two . . . we recordin'?
I'm cancerous, so when I dis you wouldn't wanna answer this
If you responded back with a battle rap you wrote for Canibus
I'll strangle you to death then I'll choke you again
And break your fuckin' legs till your bones poke through your skin
You beef wit' me, I'ma even the score equally
Take you on Jerry Springer, and beat yer ass legally
I get too blunted off of funny homegrown
'Cause when I smoke out I hit the trees harder than Sonny Bono
(Ohh no!!) So if I said I never did drugs
That would mean I lie AND get fucked more than the president does
Hillary Clinton tried to slap me and call me a pervert

I ripped her fuckin' tonsils out and fed her sherbet (Bitch!)
My nerves hurt, and lately I'm on edge
Grabbed Vanilla Ice and ripped out his blond dreads (Fuck you!)
Every girl I ever went out wit' has gone lez
Follow me and do exactly what the song says:
Smoke weed, take pills, drop outta school, kill people and drink
Then jump behind the wheel like it was still legal
I'm dumb enough to walk in a store and steal
So I'm dumb enough to ask for a date with Lauryn Hill
Some people only see that I'm white, ignorin' skill
'Cause I stand out like a green hat with a orange bill
But I don't get pissed, y'all don't even see through the mist
How the fuck can I be white, I don't even exist
I get a clean shave, bathe, go to a rave
Die from an overdose and dig myself up out of my grave
My middle finger won't go down, how do I wave?
And this is how I'm supposed to teach kids how to behave?

Now follow me and do exactly what you see
Don't you wanna grow up to be just like me!
I slap women and eat 'shrooms, then O.D.
Now don't you wanna grow up to be just like me!

Me and Marcus Allen was butt fuckin' Nicole
When we heard a knock at the door, must have
been Ron Gold'
Jumped behind the door, put the orgy on hold
Killed 'em both and smeared blood in a white
Bronco (We did it!)
My mind won't work if my spine don't jerk
I slapped Garth Brooks out of his rhinestone shirt
I'm not a player just a ill rhyme sayer
That'll spray an aerosol can up at the ozone layer
[psssssssh]
My rap style's warped, I'm runnin' out the morgue
Witcha dead grandmother's corpse to throw it on
your porch
Jumped in a Chickenhawk cartoon wit' a cape on
And beat up Foghorn Leghorn with an acorn
I'm 'bout as normal as Norman Bates, with defor-
mative traits
Of premature birth that was four minutes late

Mother . . . are you there? I love you
I never meant to hit you over the head with
that shovel
Will someone explain to my brain that I just severed
A main vein with a chainsaw and I'm in pain?
I take a breather and sigh; either I'm high or I'm
nuts
'Cause if you ain't tiltin' this room, neither am I
So when you see your mom with a thermometer
shoved in her ass
Then it probably is obvious I got it on with her
'Cause when I drop this solo shit it's over with
I bought Cage's tape, opened it, and dubbed over it

I came to the club drunk with a fake ID
Don't you wanna grow up to be just like me!
I've been with ten women who got HIV
Now don't you wanna grow up to be just like me!
I got genital warts and it burns when I pee
Don't you wanna grow up to be just like me!
I'll tie a rope around my penis and jump from a tree
You probably wanna grow up to be just like me!!!

GUILTY

 Dre and I were in the gym one day, and we was talkin' about song concepts and shit. Dre said that we should do a song together called "Night 'n' Day," where everything he was sayin', I was sayin' the complete opposite. So I thought about it, went home that same night, and wrote it. I came back a couple of days later and told him I had the song, so he booked our studio time. The ill shit is, he did the beat the same day, so we recorded the

[sound of static]

[ANNOUNCER]
Meet Eddie, twenty-three years old.
Fed up with life and the way things are going,
He decides to rob a liquor store.
("I can't take this no more, I can't take it no
more, homes")
But on his way in, he has a sudden change of heart.

And suddenly his conscience comes into play . . .
("Shit is mine, I gotta do this . . . gotta do this")

[DR. DRE]
All right, stop! (Huh?)
Now before you walk in the door of this liquor store

FEATURING DR. DRE
CONSCIENCE

song right then. I laid down some "dummy vocals" while Dre learned his parts and we cranked it out . . . a week later. We actually did the skit part first. We hired an announcer from a talent agency to come in and do the part of "Meet such-such." We left a time length of eight bars for each skit. The announcer came in, did his thing, and we put the sound effects up underneath. We told him his parts and what he had to say, and we made the skit around what he said. Cool, huh?

And try to get money out the drawer
You better think of the consequence (But who are you?)
I'm your motherfuckin' conscience

[EMINEM]
That's nonsense!
Go in and gaffle the money and run to one of your aunt's cribs
And borrow a damn dress, and one of her blond wigs
Tell her you need a place to stay

You'll be safe for days if you shave your legs with Rene's razor blade

[DR. DRE]
Yeah, but if it all goes through like it's supposed to
The whole neighborhood knows you and they'll

expose you
Think about it before you walk in the door first
Look at the store clerk, she's older than George Burns

[EMINEM]
Fuck that! Do that shit! Shoot that bitch!
Can you afford to blow this shit? Are you that rich?
Why you give a fuck if she dies? Are you that bitch?
Do you really think she gives a fuck if you have kids?

[DR. DRE]
Man, don't do it, it's not worth it to risk it! (You're right!)
Not over this shit. (Stop!) Drop the biscuit. (I will!)
Don't even listen to Slim yo, he's bad for you
(You know what Dre? I don't like your attitude . . .)

[sound of static]

("It's all right, c'mon, just come in here for a minute")
("Mmm, I don't know!")
("Look, baby . . . ")
("Damn!")
("Yo, it's gonna be all right, right?")
("Well okay . . . ")

[ANNOUNCER]
Meet Stan, twenty-one years old. ("Give me a kiss!")
After meeting a young girl at a rave party,
Things start getting hot and heavy in an upstairs bedroom
Once again, his conscience comes into play . . . ("Shit!")

[EMINEM]
Now listen to me, while you're kissin' her cheek
And smearin' her lipstick, slip this in her drink
Now all you gotta do is nibble on this little bitch's earlobe . . .
(Yo! This girl's only fifteen years old
You shouldn't take advantage of her, that's not fair)
Yo, look at her bush . . . does it got hair? (Uh-huh!)
Fuck this bitch right here on the spot bare
Till she passes out and she forgot how she got there
(Man, ain't you ever seen that one movie *Kids*?)
No, but I seen the porno with SunDoobiest!
(Shit, you wanna get hauled off to jail?)
Man, fuck that, hit that shit raw dawg and bail . . .

[sound of static]
[pickup idling, radio playing]

[ANNOUNCER]
Meet Grady, a twenty-nine-year-old construction worker
After coming home from a hard day's work
He walks in the door of his trailer park home
To find his wife in bed with another man
("WHAT THE FUCK?!?!")
("Grady!!")

[DR. DRE]
All right, calm down, relax, start breathin' . . .

[EMINEM]
Fuck that shit, you just caught this bitch cheatin'
While you at work she's with some dude tryin' to get off?!
FUCK slittin' her throat, CUT THIS BITCH'S HEAD OFF!!!

[DR. DRE]
Wait! What if there's an explanation for this shit?
(What? She tripped? Fell? Landed on his dick?!)

BLONDE
055

All right, Shady, maybe he's right, Grady
But think about the baby before you get all crazy

[EMINEM]
Okay! Thought about it, still wanna stab her?
Grab her by the throat, get your daughter and kidnap her?
That's what I did, be smart, don't be a retard
You gonna take advice from somebody who slapped DEE BARNES??!

[DR. DRE]
What'chu say?
(What's wrong? Didn't think I'd remember?)
I'ma kill you motherfucker!

[EMINEM]
Uhhh-aahh! Temper, temper!
Mr. Dre? Mr. N.W.A?
Mr. AK comin' straight outta Compton y'all better make way?
How in the fuck you gonna tell this man not to be violent?

[DR. DRE]
'Cause he don't need to go the same route that I went
Been there, done that . . . aw fuck it . . . What am I sayin'?
Shoot 'em both Grady where's your gun at?

[gun fires, is cocked, and refired]

THE KIDS

Replaced "Kim" on the CLEAN VERSION of *The Marshall Mathers LP*

[MR. MACKEY]
And everyone should get along . . .
Okay children quiet down, quiet down
Children, I'd like to introduce our new substitute teacher for the day
His name is Mr. Shady
Children quiet down please
Brian don't throw that (SHUT UP!)
Mr. Shady will be your new substitute
While Mr. Kaniff is out with pneumonia (HE'S GOT AIDS!)
Good luck Mr. Shady

Hi there, little boys and girls (FUCK YOU!)
Today we're gonna learn how to poison squirrels
But first I'd like you meet my friend Bob (Huh?)
Say, Hi Bob! ("Hi Bob") Bob's thirty and still lives with his mom
And he don't got a job, 'cause Bob sits at home and smokes pot
But his twelve-year-old brother looks up to him an awful lot
And Bob likes to hang out at the local waffle spot
And wait in the parkin' lot for waitresses off the clock
When it's late and the lot gets dark and fake like he walks his dog
Drag 'em in the woods and go straight to the chopping block (AHH!)
And even if they escaped and they got the cops
The ladies would all be so afraid, they would drop the charge

Till one night Mrs. Stacey went off the job
When she felt someone grab her whole face and said not to talk
But Stacey knew it was Bob and said knock it off
But Bob wouldn't knock it off 'cause he's crazy and off his rocker
Crazier than Slim Shady is off the vodka
You couldn't even take him to Dre's and get Bob a "Dr."
He grabbed Stace by the leg and chopped it off her
And dropped her off in the lake for the cops to find her
But ever since the day Stacey went off to wander
They never found her, and Bob still hangs at the waffle diner
And that's the story of Bob and his marijuana
And what it might do to you
So see if the squirrels want any—it's bad for you

CHORUS:
SEE CHILDREN, DRUGS ARE BAHHHD (C'MON)
AND IF YOU DON'T BELIEVE ME, ASK YA DAHHHD (ASK HIM, MAN)
AND IF YOU DON'T BELIEVE HIM, ASK YA MOM (THAT'S RIGHT)
SHE'LL TELL YOU HOW SHE DOES 'EM ALL THE TIME (SHE WILL)
SO KIDS SAY NO TO DRUGS (THAT'S RIGHT)
SO YOU DON'T ACT LIKE EVERYONE ELSE DOES (UH-HUH)
THEN THERE'S REALLY NOTHIN' ELSE TO SAY (SING ALONG)
DRUGS ARE JUST BAD, MMM'KAY?

My penis is the size of a peanut, have you seen it?
FUCK NO you ain't seen it, it's the size of a peanut (Huh?)
Speakin' of peanuts, you know what else is bad for squirrels?
Ecstasy is the worst drug in the world
If someone ever offers it to you, don't do it
Kids two hits'll probably drain all your spinal fluid
And spinal fluid is final, you won't get it back
So don't get attached, it'll attack every bone in your back
Meet Zach, twenty-one years old
After hangin' out with some friends at a frat party, he gets bold
And decides to try five, when he's bribed by five guys
And peer pressure will win every time you try to fight it
Suddenly he starts to convulse and his pulse goes into hyperdrive
And his eyes roll back in his skull [blblblblblb]
His back starts ta look like the McDonald's arches
He's on Donald's carpet, layin' horizontal barfin'

[BLEH]

And everyone in the apartment starts laughin' at him
"Hey Adam, Zach is a jackass, look at him!"
'Cause they took it too, so they think it's funny
So they're laughing at basically nothing except maybe wasting his money
Meanwhile, Zach's in a coma, the action is over
And his back and his shoulders hunched up like he's practicin' yoga
And that's the story of Zach, the Ecstasy maniac
So don't even feed that to squirrels, class, 'cause it's bad for you

CHORUS:
SEE CHILDREN, DRUGS ARE BAHHHD (THAT'S RIGHT)
AND IF YOU DON'T BELIEVE ME, ASK YA DAHHHD (THAT'S RIGHT)
AND IF YOU DON'T BELIEVE HIM, ASK YA MOM (YOU CAN)
SHE'LL TELL YOU HOW SHE DOES 'EM ALL THE TIME (SHE WILL)
SO KIDS SAY NO TO DRUGS (SMOKE CRACK)
SO YOU DON'T ACT LIKE EVERYONE ELSE DOES (THAT'S RIGHT)
AND THERE'S REALLY NOTHIN' ELSE TO SAY (BUT UMM)
DRUGS ARE JUST BAD, MMM'KAY?

And last but not least, one of the most humongous
Problems among young people today is fungus
It grows from cow manure, they pick it out, wipe it off,
Bag it up, and you put it right in your mouth and chew it
Yum yum!
Then you start to see some dumb stuff
And everything slows down when you eat some of 'em . . .
And sometimes you see things that aren't there
(Like what?)
Like fat women in G-strings with orange hair
(Mr. Shady, what's a G-string?) It's yarn, Claire
Women stick 'em up their behinds, go out and wear 'em (Huh?)
And if you swallow too much of the magic mushrooms
Whoops, did I say magic mushrooms? I meant fungus

Ya tongue gets all swoll up like a cow's tongue
(How come?)
'Cause it comes from a cow's dump
(Gross!!)
See, drugs are bad, it's a common fact
But your mom and dad know that's all that I'm good at (Oh!)
But don't be me, 'cause if you grow up and you go and OD
They're gonna come for me and I'ma have to grow a goatee
And get a disguise and hide, 'cause it'll be my fault
So don't do drugs, and do exactly as I don't,
'Cause I'm bad for you

CHORUS:
SEE CHILDREN, DRUGS ARE BAHHHD (UH-HUH)
AND IF YOU DON'T BELIEVE ME, ASK YA DAHHHD (PUT THAT DOWN)
AND IF YOU DON'T BELIEVE HIM, ASK YA MOM (YOU CAN ASK)
SHE'LL TELL YOU HOW SHE DOES 'EM ALL THE TIME (AND SHE WILL)
SO KIDS SAY NO TO DRUGS (SAY NO)
SO YOU DON'T ACT LIKE EVERYONE ELSE DOES (LIKE I DO)
AND THERE'S REALLY NOTHIN' ELSE TO SAY (THAT'S RIGHT)
DRUGS ARE JUST BAD, MMM'KAY?

[MR. MACKEY]
Come on, children, clap along
(SHUT UP!)
Sing along, children (Suck my motherfuckin' dick!)
Drugs are just bad, drugs are just bad (*South Park* is gonna sue me!)
So don't do drugs (Suck my motherfuckin' penis!)
So there'll be more for me (Hippie! Goddamnit!)
(Mushrooms killed Kenny! [fart] Ewww, ahhh!)
(So fucked up right now . . .)

MARSHALL

While putting together my second album, I kind of wanted to come up with an "I Don't Give a Fuck," Part 3. Jeff from FBT was playin' this acoustic guitar track. He then started singing the hook "'Cause I'm just Marshall Mathers." It's ill, because every time we're fucking around in the studio we seem to come up with the dopest shit. We'll fuck around and be smiling while we're sayin' shit and I'll say, "Yo, that's dope. I should use that." When I thought of the chorus, I felt that what I needed to talk about in the

You know I just don't get it
Last year I was nobody
This year I'm sellin' records
Now everybody wants to come around like I owe 'em somethin'
Heh, the fuck you want from me, ten million dollars?
Get the fuck out of here

CHORUS ONE:
YOU SEE, I'M JUST MARSHALL MATHERS (MARSHALL MATHERS)
I'M JUST A REGULAR GUY
I DON'T KNOW WHY ALL THE FUSS ABOUT ME (FUSS ABOUT ME)
NOBODY EVER GAVE A FUCK BEFORE
ALL THEY DID WAS DOUBT ME (DID WAS DOUBT ME)
NOW EVERYBODY WANNA RUN THEY MOUTH
AND TRY TO TAKE SHOTS AT ME (TAKE SHOTS AT ME)

MATHERS

verses was just me and my opinions. So I touched on everything from the newest trends in hip-hop (which I'm not really with), to ICP, to my mother, to my family members who don't know me and always wanna come around. I wanted to just spit fire in each verse and have that soft-ass innocent chorus. I think it captures the whole "front porch" feel depicted on the album's cover. When I recorded this I decided to call the album *The Marshall Mathers LP*.

Yo, you might see me joggin', you might see me walkin'
You might see me walkin' a dead rottweiler dog
With its head chopped off in the park with a spiked collar
Hollerin' at him 'cause the son of a bitch won't quit barkin' (grrrr, ARF ARF)
Or leanin' out a window, with a cocked shotgun
Drivin' up the block in the car that they shot 'Pac in
Lookin' for Big's killers, dressin' ridiculous
Blue and red like I don't see what the big deal is
Double-barrel twelve-gauge bigger than Chris Wallace
Pissed off, 'cause Biggie and 'Pac just missed all this
Watchin' all these cheap imitations get rich off 'em
And get dollars that shoulda been theirs like they switched wallets
And amidst all this Crist' poppin' and wristwatches
I just sit back and just watch and just get nauseous
And walk around with an empty bottle of Rémy Martin

Startin' shit like some twenty-six-year-old skinny
Cartman ("Goddamnit!")
I'm anti-Backstreet and Ricky Martin
With instincts to kill N'Sync, don't get me started
These fuckin' brats can't sing and Britney's garbage
What's this bitch, retarded? Gimme back my
sixteen dollars
All I see is sissies in magazines smiling
Whatever happened to whylin' out and bein' violent?
Whatever happened to catchin' a good ol'-fashioned
Passionate ass-whoopin' and gettin' your shoes,
coat, and your hat tooken?
New Kids on the Block sucked a lot of dick
Boy/girl groups make me sick
And I can't wait till I catch all you faggots in public
I'ma love it . . . (hahaha)
Vanilla Ice don't like me (uh-uh)
Said some shit in *Vibe* to spite me (yup)
Then went and dyed his hair just like me (hehe)
A bunch of little kids wanna swear just like me
And run around screamin', "I don't care, just bite
me" (nah nah)
I think I was put here to annoy the world
And destroy your little four-year-old boy or girl
Plus I was put here to put fear in faggots who
spray Faygo Root Beer

And call themselves "Clowns" 'cause they look queer
Faggy 2 Dope and Silent Gay
Claimin' Detroit, when y'all live twenty miles away
(fuckin' punks)
And I don't wrestle, I'll knock you fuckin' faggots
the fuck out
Ask 'em about the club they was at when they
snuck out
After they ducked out the back when they saw us
and bugged out
(AHHH!) Ducked down and got paint balls shot at
they truck, blaow!
Look at y'all runnin' your mouth again
When you ain't seen a fuckin' Mile Road South of 10
And I don't need help, from D-12, to beat up two
females
In makeup, who may try to scratch me with Lee
Nails
"Slim Anus," you damn right, Slim Anus
I don't get fucked in mine like you two little flam-
ing faggots!

CHORUS TWO:
'CAUSE I'M JUST MARSHALL MATHERS
(MARSHALL MATHERS)
I'M NOT A WRESTLER GUY,

I'LL KNOCK YOU OUT IF YOU TALK ABOUT ME
(YOU TALK ABOUT ME)
COME AND SEE ME ON THE STREETS ALONE
IF YOU ASSHOLES DOUBT ME (ASSHOLES
DOUBT ME)
AND IF YOU WANNA RUN YOUR MOUTH
THEN COME TAKE YOUR BEST SHOT AT ME (YOUR
BEST SHOT AT ME)

Is it because you love me that y'all expect so much
of me?
You little groupie bitch, get off me, go fuck Puffy
Now because of this blond mop that's on top of
this fucked-up head that I've got, I've gone pop?
The underground just spunned around and did a 360
Now these kids dis me and act like some big sissies
"Oh, he just did some shit with Missy,
So now he thinks he's too big to do some shit with
MC Get-Bizzy"
My fuckin' bitch mom is suin' for ten million
She must want a dollar for every pill I've been stealin'
Shit, where the fuck you think I picked up the habit?
All I had to do was go in her room and lift up
a mattress
Which is it, bitch, Mrs. Briggs or Ms. Mathers?
It doesn't matter you faggot!

Talkin' about I fabricated my past
He's just aggravated I won't ejaculate in his ass
(Uhh!)
So tell me, what the hell is a fella to do?
For every million I make, another relative sues
Family fightin' and fussin' over who wants to invite
me to supper
All of a sudden, I got ninety-some cousins (Hey
it's me!)
A half brother and sister who never seen me
Or even bothered to call me until they saw me on TV
Now everybody's so happy and proud
I'm finally allowed to step foot in my girlfriend's house
Hey-hey! And then to top it off, I walk to the
newsstand
To buy this cheap-ass little magazine with a
food stamp
Skip to the last page, flip right fast
And what do I see? A picture of my big white ass
Okay, let me give you motherfuckers some help:
Uhh, here—DOUBLE XL, DOUBLE XL
Now your magazine shouldn't have so much
trouble to sell
Ahh fuck it, I'll even buy a couple myself

CHORUS ONE (2X)

CRIMINAL

After I did "Marshall Mathers," I felt like I still hadn't captured that "Still Don't Give a Fuck" feel. I played it for my manager, Paul, and he said, "It's dope, but it's still not 'Give a Fuck'." Once again, the funniest shit happens when I'm about to bail. We were about to leave the studio for the day, 'cause we couldn't come up with shit. Jeff was in the next studio playin' with this old-ass piano. He was playin' the frantic piano loop that gave "Criminal" that sinister feel. All I had was "I'm a Criminal." I hadn't filled the blanks in yet. So I started writing the rhyme and within twenty minutes we were on our way out the door with a hook and the first two verses in hand. I went home and finished the last verse. Afterwards, I put in the skit right before the album was finished. Only fucked-up thing was that it took almost a whole day to do that bank robbery skit. Even Dre walked out of the studio like "Fuck it, I'm out." We had to get Mel-Man to get his lines right, 'cause he was so drunk. He just had to say "Don't kill nobody." But what really took so long was the noise in the background. I did that skit by myself. I learned how from Dre when we hooked up on "Guilty Conscience." "Criminal" was my new "Still Don't Give a Fuck" for *The Marshall Mathers LP*. That's why I did the same intro as I did on "Still Don't." That's why—just like "Still Don't Give a Fuck"—it's the last song on the record. It sums up the whole album.

A lot of people ask me . . . stupid fuckin' questions
A lot of people think that . . . what I say on records
Or what I talk about on a record, that I actually do in real life
Or that I believe in it
Or if I say that I wanna kill somebody, that . . .
I'm actually gonna do it
Or that I believe in it
Well, shit . . . if you believe that then I'll kill you
You know why? 'Cause I'm a

    CRIMINAL
    CRIMINAL
    YOU GODDAMN RIGHT
    I'M A CRIMINAL
    YEAH, I'M A CRIMINAL

My words are like a dagger with a jagged edge
That'll stab you in the head whether you're a fag or lez
Or the homosex, hermaph, or a trans-a-vest

Pants or dress—hate fags? The answer's "yes"
Homophobic? Nah, you're just heterophobic
Starin' at my jeans, watchin' my genitals bulgin' (Ooh!)
That's my motherfuckin' balls, you'd better let go of 'em
They belong in my scrotum, you'll never get hold of 'em
Hey, it's me, Versace
Whoops, somebody shot me!
And I was just checkin' the mail
Get it? Checkin' the "male"?
How many records you expectin' to sell
After your second LP sends you directly to jail?
C'mon!—Relax guy, I like gay men
Right, Ken? Give me an amen (AAA-men!)
Please Lord, this boy needs Jesus
Heal this child, help us destroy these demons
Oh, and please send me a brand-new car
And a prostitute while my wife's sick in the hospital
Preacher, preacher, fifth-grade teacher
You can't reach me, my mom can't neither
You can't teach me a goddamn thing 'cause
I watch TV, and Comcast cable
And you ain't able to stop these thoughts

You can't stop me from toppin' these charts
And you can't stop me from droppin' each March
With a brand-new CD for these fuckin' retards
Duhhh, and to think, it's just little ol' me
Mr. "Don't Give a Fuck" still won't leave

CHORUS (REPEAT 2X):

I'm a CRIMINAL
'Cause every time I write a rhyme, these people think it's a crime
To tell 'em what's on my mind—I guess I'm a CRIMINAL
But I don't gotta say a word, I just flip 'em the bird
And keep goin', I don't take shit from no one

The mother did drugs—hard liquor, cigarettes, and speed
The baby came out—disfigured, ligaments indeed
It was a seed who would grow up just as crazy as she
Don't dare make fun of that baby 'cause that baby was me
I'm a CRIMINAL—an animal caged who turned crazed
But how the fuck you s'posed to grow up when you weren't raised?

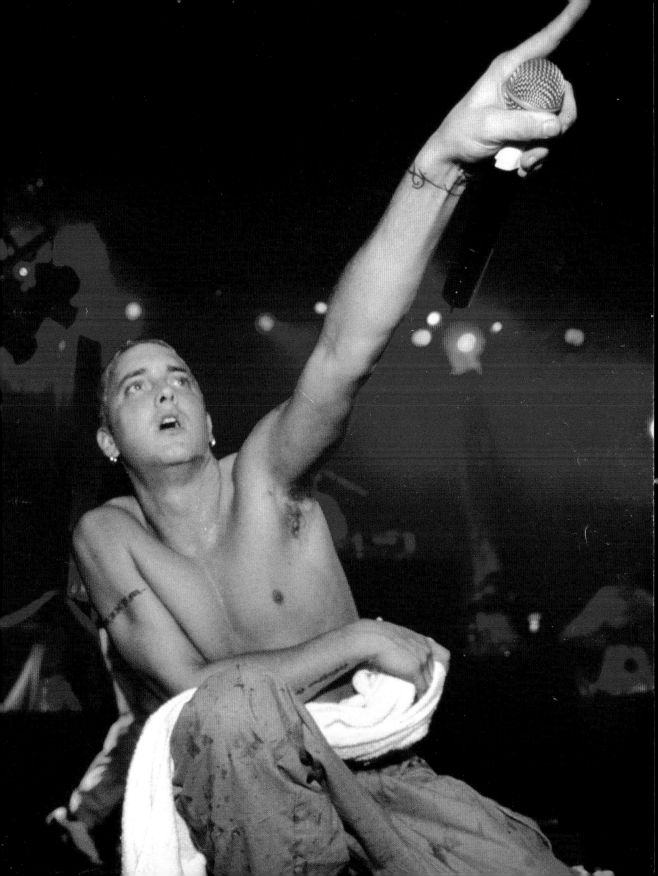

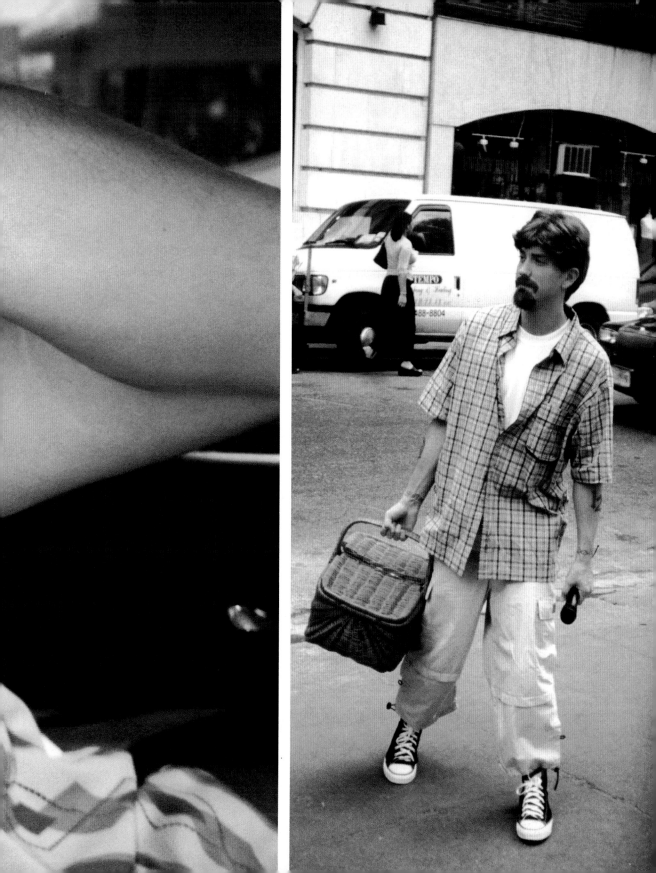

So as I got older and I got a lot taller
My dick shrunk smaller, but my balls got larger
I drank more liquor to fuck you up quicker
Than you'd wanna fuck me up for sayin' the word . . .
My morals went *thhbbpp* when the President got oral
Sex in his Oval Office on top of his desk
Off of his own employee
Now don't ignore me, you won't avoid me
You can't miss me, I'm white, blond-haired
And my nose is pointy
I'm the bad guy who makes fun of people that die
In plane crashes and laughs
As long as it ain't happenin' to him
Slim Shady, I'm as crazy as Em-
inem and Kim combined—[kch] the maniac's in
Place of the doctor 'cause Dre couldn't make it today
He's a little under the weather, so I'm takin' his place
(Mm-mm-mmm!) Oh, that's Dre with an AK to his face
Don't make me kill him too and spray his brains all over the place
I told you, Dre, you should've kept that thang put away
I guess that'll teach you not to let me play with it, eh?
I'm a CRIMINAL

[INTERLUDE SKIT]

Aight look (uh-huh) just go up in that motherfucker get
the motherfuckin' money and get the fuck up outta there
[EMINEM] Aight
I'll be right here waitin' on you
[EMINEM] Aight
Yo Em
[EMINEM] What?!
Don't kill nobody this time
[EMINEM] Awwright . . . goddamn, fuck . . .
(whistling) How you doin'?
[TELLER] Hi, how can I help you?
[EMINEM] Yeah, I need to make a withdrawal

[TELLER] Okay
[EMINEM] Put the fuckin' money in the bag, bitch, and I won't kill you!
[TELLER] What? Oh my God, don't kill me
[EMINEM] I'm not gonna kill you, bitch, quit lookin' around . . .
[TELLER] Don't kill me, please don't kill me . . .
[EMINEM] I said I'm not gonna fuckin' kill you
Hurry the fuck up! [BOOM] Thank you!

Windows tinted on my ride when I drive in it
So when I rob a bank, run out and just dive in it
So I'll be disguised in it
And if anybody identifies the guy in it
I hide for five minutes
Come back, shoot the eyewitness
And fire at the private eye hired to pry in my business
Die, bitches, bastards, brats, pets
This puppy's lucky I didn't blast his ass yet
If I ever gave a fuck, I'd shave my nuts
Tuck my dick in between my legs and cluck
You motherfuckin' chickens ain't brave enough
To say the stuff I say, so this tape is shut
Shit, half the shit I say, I just make it up
To make you mad, so kiss my white naked ass
And if it's not a rapper that I make it as
I'ma be a fuckin' rapist in a Jason mask

(Chorus 2X)

INTRO (8 / 9 NOWS)
KILL U (1VERSE / 1 CHORUS)
DEAD WRONG (2 MUSIC / 2 ACCAPELLA)
JUST DON'T GIVE A (1VERSE / 1CHORUS)
ROLE MODEL (1VERSE / 1 CHORUS)

MY NAME IS (1VERSE / 1 CHORUS)
MARSHALL MATHERS (1VERSE/1CHORUS)
CRIMINAL (1VERSE / 1CHORUS)

I AM (1VERSE / 1 CHORUS)
STILL DON'T GIVE A (1VERSE/ 1CHORUS)

REAL SLIM SHADY

love,
Slim Shady
J- 12

AS THE WORLD TURNS

The first verse on "As the World Turns" was based on this fat chick I used to fight with in gym class. We used to have swimming every Wednesday. There was this big, fat, butch-type chick. Like a female bully that used to fuck with me. I can't remember her name, but I used to argue with her a lot. But that's where the first verse kind of stems from. The line about "taking a girl up to the highest diving board and tossing her over" and shit like that. Then, the second verse kind of fit the whole drawing that my boy Skam had drawn on the inside of my album cover. I captured that whole trailer-park-white-trash type of setup. I just wanted to make a funny story. I didn't even know the first verse and the second verse were going into the same song. Just like "Brain Damage," I wrote the first verse before I got a deal, second verse once I got the deal. I was gonna throw the first verse out. It was going to be one of those freestyle verses that I drop for college radio. But when I thought of the hook I was like "Yo, this what I'ma do. I'm gonna put these two verses together." So then we just went and did the beat.

BLONDE

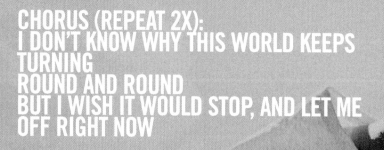

CHORUS (REPEAT 2X):
I DON'T KNOW WHY THIS WORLD KEEPS TURNING
ROUND AND ROUND
BUT I WISH IT WOULD STOP, AND LET ME OFF RIGHT NOW

Yes man
As the World Turns
We all experience things in life
Trials and Tribulations
That we all must go through
When someone wants to test us
When someone tries our patience

I hang with a bunch of hippies and wacky tobacco planters
Who swallow lit roaches
And light up like jack-o'-lanterns
Outsidaz baby, and we sue in the courts
'Cause we're dope as fuck and only get a 2 in *The Source*

They never should've booted me out of reform school

Deformed fool, takin' a shit in a warm pool
Until they threw me out the Ramada Inn
I said it wasn't me, I got a twin (Oh my god it's you! Not again!)
It all started when my mother took my bike away
'Cause I murdered my guinea pig and stuck him in the microwave
After that, it was straight to the 40-ouncers

Slappin' teachers and jackin' off in front of my counselors
Class clown freshman, dressed like Les Nessman
Fuck the next lesson, I'll pass the test guessin'
And all the other kids said, "Eminem's a diss-head,
He'll never last, the only class he'll ever pass is phys ed"
May be true, till I told this bitch in gym class
That she was too fat to swim laps, she needed Slim-Fast (Who me?)
Yeah bitch, you so big you walked into Vic Tanny's and stepped on Jenny Craig
She picked me up to snap me like a skinny twig
Put me in a headlock, then I thought of my guinea pig
I felt the evilness and started transformin'

(RARRRR!)

It began storming, I heard a bunch of cheering fans swarming
Grabbed that bitch by her hair
Drug her across the ground
And took her up to the highest diving board
and tossed her down
Sorry, coach, it's too late to tell me stop
While I drop this bitch facedown and watch her belly flop

CHORUS

As the World Turns
These are the days of our lives
These are the things that we must go through
Day by day

We drive around in million-dollar sports cars
While little kids hide this tape from their parents like bad report cards
Outsidaz, and we sue in the courts
'Cause we dope as fuck and only get a 2 in *The Source*
Hypochondriac, hanging out at the Laundromat
Where all the raunchy fat white trashy blondes be at
Dressed like a sailor, standin' by a pail of garbage
It's almost dark and I'm still tryin' to nail a trailer-park bitch
I met a slut and said, "What up, it's nice to meet ya"

I'd like to treat ya to a Faygo and a slice of pizza
But I'm broke as fuck and I don't get paid till the first of next month
But if you care to join me, I was 'bout to roll this next blunt
But I ain't got no weed, no Phillies, or no papers
Plus I'm a rapist and a repeated prison escapist

So gimme all your money
And don't try nothin' funny

'Cause you know your stinkin' ass is too fat to try to outrun me

I went to grab my gun

That's when her ass put it on me
Wit' an uppercut and hit me with a basket of laundry
I fell through the glass doors
Started causin' a scene
Then slid across the floor and flew right into a washin' machine
Jumped up with a broken back
Thank God I was smokin' crack all day
And doped up off coke and smack
All I wanted to do was rape the bitch and snatch her purse

Now I wanna kill her

But yo I gotta catch her first
Ran through Rally's parkin' lot and took a shortcut

Saw the house she ran up in
And shot her fuckin' porch up
Kicked the door down to murder this divorced slut

Looked around the room
That's when I seen the bedroom door shut
I know you're in there, bitch! I got my gun cocked!
You might as well come out now
She said, "Come in, it's unlocked!"
I walked in and all I smelled was Liz Claiborne
And seen her spread across the bed naked watchin' gay porn
She said, "Come here, big boy, let's get acquainted"

I turned around to run, twisted my ankle and sprained it
She came at me at full speed, nothin' could stop her
I shot her five times and every bullet bounced off her
I started to beg, "No, please let go"
But she swallowed my fuckin' leg whole like an egg roll
With one leg left, now I'm hoppin' around crippled
I grabbed my pocketknife and sliced off her right nipple
Just trying to buy me some time, then I remembered this magic trick
Den Den Den Den Den Den, go go gadget dick!
Whipped that shit out, and ain't no doubt about it
It hit the ground and caused an earthquake and power outage
I shouted, "Now bitch, let's see who gets the best!"
Stuffed that shit in crooked and fucked that fat slut to death

(Ahh!! Ahhh!)

Come here, bitch!
Come here!
Take this motherfuckin' dick!
Bitch, come here!

    CHORUS TO FADE

And as we go along
Throughout the days of our lives
We all face small obstacles and challenges every day
That we must go through
These are the things that surround us through our atmosphere

Every day
Every single day the world
keeps turning

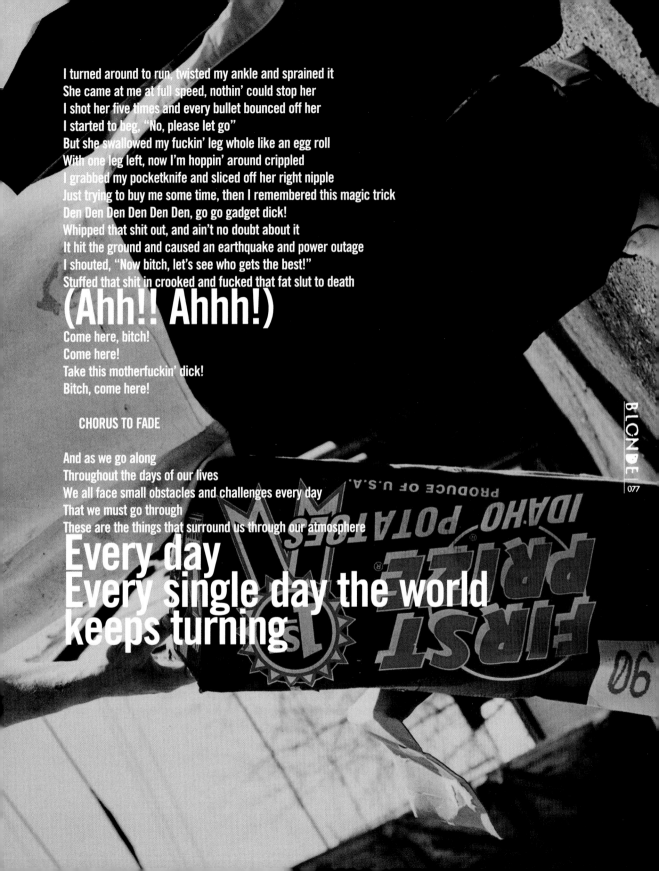

This little media favorite was actually the first official song that I wrote for the album. I had completed it back in '98, when the first album was done. I wrote this song when Kim and I weren't together. We were broken up at the time. This was the end of '98. I remember I was watchin' a movie one day that inspired me to write a love song, but I didn't want to make a corny love song. It had to be some bugged-out shit. Though I don't remember what movie it was, I do remember feeling the frustration of us breaking up and having a daughter all in the mix. I really wanted to pour my heart out, but yet, I also wanted to scream. I didn't want to say, "Baby, I love you, come back to me," and all that crap. I wanted to fuckin' scream. So the same day I went to the flick, I went back to the studio and once again walked into a session with the perfect beat already playing. Surprisingly enough,

"Kim" was the only track on the album that I had nothing to do with in terms of pro-
duction. FBT created that track and they had it ready for me in the studio. When I started
writing the song, I thought that maybe I could tie it into "'97 Bonnie and Clyde." So I
decided to make it a prequel. You never would've thought, but I played it for her once
we started talking again. I asked her to tell me what she thought of it. I remember my dumb-ass saying "I know this is a fucked-up song, but it shows how much I care about you. To even think about
you this much. To even put you on a song like this." I did the vocals in one take. The mood I
wanted to capture was that of an argument that me and her would have, and judging from the attention the media has given this song, you can see that's exactly what I did . . . and then some.

BLONDE

079

Aww look at daddy's baby girl
That's daddy baby
Little sleepyhead
Yesterday I changed your diaper
Wiped you and powdered you
How did you get so big?
Can't believe it now you're two
Baby, you're so precious
Daddy's so proud of you
Sit down bitch
You move again
I'll beat the shit out of you
(Okay)
Don't make me wake this baby

She don't need to see what I'm about to do

Quit crying, bitch, why do you always make me shout at you?
How could you? Just leave me and love him out of the blue
Aw, what's a matter Kim?
Am I too loud for you?
Too bad, bitch, you're gonna finally hear me out this time
At first, I'm like all right
You wanna throw me out? That's fine!
But not for him to take my place, are you out your mind?
This couch, this TV, this whole house is mine!
How could you let him sleep in our bed?
Look at me, Kim
Look at your husband now!
(No!)
I said look at him!
He ain't so hot now is he?
Little punk!
(Why are you doing this?)
Shut the fuck up!

(You're drunk! You're never gonna get away at this!)
You think I give a fuck!
Come on we're going for a ride bitch
(No!)
Sit up front
(We can't just leave Hailie alone, what if she wakes up?)
We'll be right back
Well, I will—you'll be in the trunk

CHORUS:
SO LONG, BITCH YOU DID ME SO WRONG
I DON'T WANNA GO ON
LIVING IN THIS WORLD WITHOUT YOU

(REPEAT)

You really fucked me, Kim
You really did a number on me
I never knew me cheating on you would come back to haunt me
But we was kids then, Kim, I was only eighteen
That was years ago
I thought we wiped the slate clean
That's fucked up!
(I love you!)
Oh God my brain is racing
(I love you!)
What are you doing?
Change the station I hate this song!
Does this look like a big joke?
(No!)

There's a four-year-old boy lyin' dead with a slit throat In your living room, ha-ha

What you think I'm kiddin' you?

You loved him didn't you?

(No!)

Bullshit, you bitch, don't fucking lie to me
What the fuck's this guy's problem on the side of me?
Fuck you, asshole, yeah bite me
Kim, KIM!
Why don't you like me?
You think I'm ugly don't you
(It's not that!)
No, you think I'm ugly
(Baby)
Get the fuck away from me, don't touch me
I HATE YOU! I HATE YOU!
I SWEAR TO GOD I HATE YOU
OH MY GOD I LOVE YOU
How the fuck could you do this to me?
(Sorry!)
How the fuck could you do this to me?

CHORUS (2X)

Come on, get out
(I can't I'm scared)
I said get out, bitch!
(Let go of my hair, please don't do this, baby)
(Please, I love you, look we can just take Hailie and leave)
Fuck you, you did this to us
You did it, it's your fault
Oh my God I'm crackin' up
Get a grip Marshall
Hey, remember the time we went to Brian's party?

And you were like so drunk that you threw up all over Archie
That was funny wasn't it?
(Yes!)
That was funny wasn't it?
(Yes!)
See, it all makes sense, doesn't it?
You and your husband have a fight
One of you tries to grab a knife
And during the struggle he accidentally gets his Adam's apple sliced
(No!)
And while this is goin' on
His son is woke up and he walks in
She panics and he gets his throat cut
(Oh my God!)
So now they both dead and you slash your own throat
So now it's double homicide and suicide with no note
I should have known better when you started to act weird
We could've . . . HEY! Where you going? Get back here!
You can't run from me, Kim
It's just us, nobody else!
You're only making this harder on yourself
Ha! Ha! Gotcha!
(Ahh!)
Ha! Go ahead, yell! Here, I'll scream with you!
AH SOMEBODY HELP!
Don't you get it, bitch, no one can hear you?
Now shut the fuck up and get what's comin' to you
You were supposed to love me
[Kim choking]

NOW BLEED! BITCH, BLEED! BLEED! BITCH, BLEED! BLEED!

CHORUS (2X)

AMITYVILLE

I wanted to make a song about Detroit, and "Amityville" was a new name I came up with for Detroit. I thought of the hook, and then I had the name. Matter of fact, we recorded "Drug Ballad" and "Amityville" the very next day. The beat was kinda slow. So I decided to put Bizzare of D-12 on the song, 'cause he sounds good over this tempo. My first verse and Bizzare's verse weren't really dealing with the theme at hand. I said, "Yo, we need to talk about Detroit." So on the last verse, I kinda summed everything up. The label was actually buggin' off of Bizzare's verse. So I knew we did it right.

(kill kill kill)
Dahh-dum, dahh-dum . . . dum
Dahh-dum, dahh-dum, duh-da-da-da-da
(kill kill kill)
Dahh-dum, dahh-dum . . . dum
Dahh-dum, dahh-dum, dumm . . .

(kill kill kill)

CHORUS:
MENTALLY ILLLL FROM AMITYVILLLLE (ILLLL)
ACCIDENTALLY KILLLL YOUR FAMILY STILLLL
THINKIN' HE WON'T? GODDAMNIT HE WILLLL
(HE'SSSS)*
MENTALLY ILLLL FROM AMITYVILLLLE
*ON REPEATS ONLY

I get lifted and spin till I'm half-twisted
Feet planted and stand with a grin full of
chapped lipstick [SMACK]
Pen full of ink, think sinful and rap sick shit
Shrink pencil me in for my last visit
Drink gin till my chin's full of splashed whiskers
[whoosh]
Hash whiskey and ash till I slap bitches [smack]
Ask Bizzy, he's been here the past six years
Mash with me again and imagine this

CHORUS 2X

That's why this city is filled with a bunch of
fuckin' idiots still (still)
That's why the first motherfucker poppin' some
shit he gets killed (killed)
That's why we don't call it Detroit,
we call it Amityville ('Ville)
You can get capped after just havin' a cavity
filled (filled)

Ahahahaha, that's why we're crowned the murder
capital still (still)
This ain't Detroit, this is motherfuckin' Hamburger
Hill! (Hill!)

We don't do drive-bys, we park in front of houses and shoot

And when the police come we fuckin' shoot it out
with them too!
That's the mentality here (here) that's the reality
here (here)
Did I just hear somebody say
they wanna challenge me here?? (huh?)
While I'm holdin' a pistol with
this many calibers here?? (here??)
Plus a registration that just made
this shit valid this year? (year?)
'Cause once I snap I can't be held
accountable for my acts
And that's when accidents happen,
When a thousand bullets
come at your house
And collapse the foundation around you
and they found you
And your family in it (AHHHHH!)
GODDAMNIT, HE MEANT IT WHEN HE TELLS YOU

CHORUS 2X

Dum, tahh-dum . . . ta-dah-da
Dum, tahh-dum . . . ta-dah-da
Dum, tahh-dum . . . ta-dah-da
Dum, tahh-dum . . . ta-dah-da
Dum, tahh-dum . . . ta-dah-da
Dum, tahh-dum . . . ta-dah-da
Dum, tahh-dum . . . ta-dah-da
Dum, tahh-dum . . . ta-dah-da
dum . . .

ANGRY

This song is just another one of those tracks that we did one day just fucking around. I wrote the rhyme in about twenty minutes. All three verses. The hook was simple. I hummed Jeff the bass line. I wanted to touch on how last year I was always fucked up. Life was like a big party for me. It was the first year that I blew up, and I did a lot of celebrating. By the way, that vocal is the same girl from "Get Down Tonight."

UG

[GIRL] YEAAAH, HAHAHAHA . . . WHOOOOO, SHIT!
[EMINEM] (AIGHT)
[EMINEM] GUESS WHAT? I AIN'T COMING IN YET . . .
I'LL COME IN A MINUTE
[EMINEM] AYO . . . THIS IS MY LOVE SONG . . . IT GOES LIKE THIS

Back when Mark Walhberg was Marky Mark
This is how we used to make the party start
We used to mix Hen' with Bacardi Dark
And when it kicks in, you can hardly talk
And by the sixth gin you're gonna probably crawl
And you'll be sick then and you'll probably barf
And my prediction is you're gonna probably fall
Either somewhere in the lobby or the hallway wall
And everything's spinning
You're beginnin' to think women
Are swimming in pink linen again in the sink

LAD

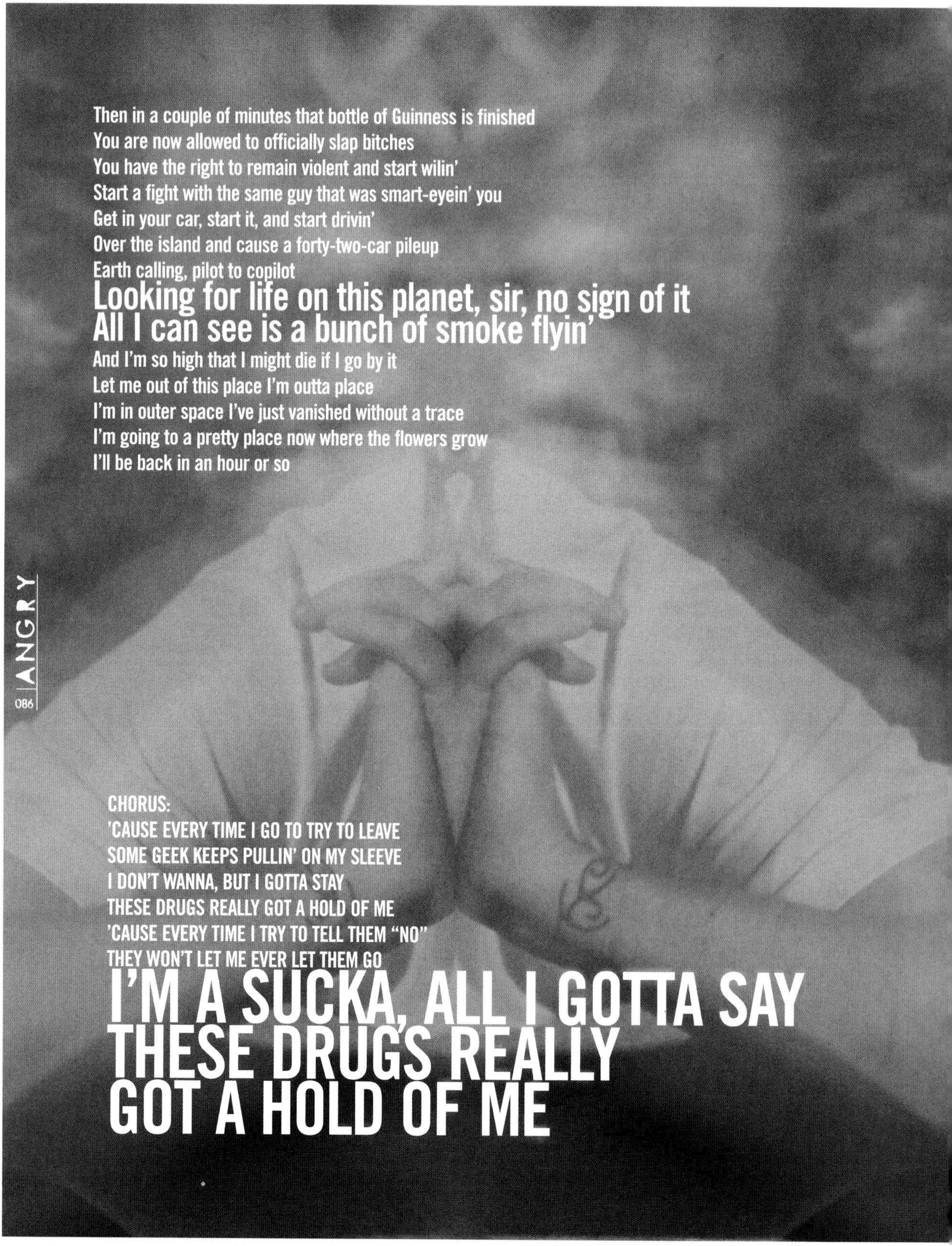

Then in a couple of minutes that bottle of Guinness is finished
You are now allowed to officially slap bitches
You have the right to remain violent and start wilin'
Start a fight with the same guy that was smart-eyein' you
Get in your car, start it, and start drivin'
Over the island and cause a forty-two-car pileup
Earth calling, pilot to copilot
Looking for life on this planet, sir, no sign of it
All I can see is a bunch of smoke flyin'
And I'm so high that I might die if I go by it
Let me out of this place I'm outta place
I'm in outer space I've just vanished without a trace
I'm going to a pretty place now where the flowers grow
I'll be back in an hour or so

ANGRY

086

CHORUS:
'CAUSE EVERY TIME I GO TO TRY TO LEAVE
SOME GEEK KEEPS PULLIN' ON MY SLEEVE
I DON'T WANNA, BUT I GOTTA STAY
THESE DRUGS REALLY GOT A HOLD OF ME
'CAUSE EVERY TIME I TRY TO TELL THEM "NO"
THEY WON'T LET ME EVER LET THEM GO
I'M A SUCKA, ALL I GOTTA SAY
THESE DRUGS REALLY
GOT A HOLD OF ME

In third grade, all I used to do
Was sniff glue through a tube and play Rubik's Cube
Seventeen years later I'm as rude as Jude
Scheming on the first chick with the hugest boobs
I've got no game

And every face looks the same
They've got no name

So I don't need game to play
I just say whatever I want to whoever I want
Whenever I want, wherever I want, however I want
However, I do show some respect to few
This Ecstacy's got me standing next to you
Getting sentimental as fuck spillin' guts to you
We just met
But I think I'm in love with you
But you're on it too

So you tell me you love me too
Wake up in the morning like "Yo, what the fuck we do?"
I gotta go, bitch
You know I've got stuff to do
'Cause if I get caught cheatin', then I'm stuck with you
But in the long run
These drugs are probably going to catch up sooner or later
But fuck it, I'm on one
So let's enjoy
Let the X destroy your spinal cord
So it's not a straight line no more
Till we walk around looking like some windup dolls
Shit sticking out of our backs like a dinosaur

Shit, six hits won't even get me high no more
So bye for now, I'm going to try to find some more

CHORUS

That's the sound of a bottle when it's hollow
When you swallow it all, wallow and drown in your sorrow
And tomorrow you're probably going to want to do it again
What's a little spinal fluid between you and a friend?
Screw it
And what's a little bit of alcohol poisoning?
And what's a little fight?
Tomorrow you'll be boys again
It's your life
Live it however you wanna
Marijuana is everywhere
Where was you brought up?
It don't matter as long as you get where you're going
'Cause none of the shit is going to mean shit where we're going
They tell you to stop, but you just sit there ignoring
Even though you wake up feeling like shit every morning
But you're young
You've got a lot of drugs to do
Girls to screw
Parties to crash
Sucks to be you
If I could take it all back now, I wouldn't
I would have did more shit that people said that I shouldn't
But I'm all grown up now and upgraded and graduated
To better drugs and updated
But I've still got a lot of growing up to do
I've still got a whole lot of throwing up to spew
But when it's all said and done I'll be forty
Before I know it with a forty on the porch telling stories
With a bottle of Jack
Two grandkids in my lap
Baby-sitting for Hailie while Hailie is out getting smashed
CHORUS

THE WAY I AM

BLONDE | 089

"The Way I Am" was one of the few tracks that I did completely by myself. I had the beat in my head before I went into the studio to lay it down. I had the rhyme and the piano loop all worked out. I had Jeff play the loop and I finished the rhyme listening to my headphone set on the way to L.A. That's why the flow is like that, 'cause all I had was the piano loop in my headphones. I wanted to do some different shit. I thought about the rhyme first. Once I got the third line I didn't want the cadence of the rhyme to stop going with the piano. Even if I took a break with rappin', I made the words echo so that they still went with the piano. The funny thing about this is that when I wrote this song I had already turned in the whole album. Problem was my label felt that I didn't have a lead-off single yet. I thought either "I'm Back" or "I Never Knew" was gonna be the single, but they nixed both of 'em. So I got frustrated and I said, "What do you want? Another 'My Name Is?'" They said, "Not exactly, it doesn't have to be that," but they were beating around the bush, because that's exactly what they really wanted. I wrote it at Kim's parents' house (of all places) right before I went back to L.A. to go record "the single" they wanted me to come with. I stayed in hotels for a month just tryin' to come up with a single. This is the song I wrote right before "The Real Slim Shady." I was about to explode, like "YO!!! WHY IS EVERYBODY STRESSING ME!!!" I was getting sued by my mother. My father was coming out of the woodwork trying to make amends and all kinds of crazy shit. Adding to the fire was the fact that I was getting shit about the Columbine reference on "I'm Back," and the label was telling me that I wasn't gonna be able to say it. My whole thing was, what is the big fuckin' deal? That shit happens all the time. Why is that topic so touchy as opposed to, say, a four-year-old kid drowning? Why isn't that considered a huge tragedy? People die in the city all the time. People get shot, people get stabbed, raped, mugged, killed, and all kinds of shit. What the fuck is the big deal with Columbine that makes it separate from any other tragedy in America? Anyway, the label wanted a single, so I gave 'em "The Way I Am," which was the complete opposite of what they requested. I was kinda rebelling against the label by letting them know they couldn't force me to do something that I didn't want to do.

WHATEVER . . . DRE, JUST LET IT RUN
AIYYO, TURN THE BEAT UP A LITTLE BIT
AIYYO . . . THIS SONG IS FOR ANYONE . . . FUCK IT
JUST SHUT UP AND LISTEN, AIYYO . . .

I sit back with this pack of Zig Zags and this bag
Of this weed it gives me the shit needed to be
The most meanest MC on this—on this Earth
And since birth I've been cursed with this curse to
just curse
And just blurt this berserk and bizarre shit that works
And it sells and it helps in itself to relieve
All this tension dispensin'
these sentences
Gettin' this stress that's
been eatin' me
recently off of this chest
And I rest again peacefully (peacefully) . . .
But at least have the decency in you
To leave me alone, when you freaks see me out
In the streets when I'm eatin'
or feedin' my daughter
To not come and speak to
me (speak to me) . . .
I don't know you and no, I don't owe you a mo-
ther-fuck-in' thing
I'm not Mr. N'Sync, I'm not what your friends think
I'm not Mr. Friendly, I can be a prick if you tempt me
My tank is on empty (is on
empty) . . .
No patience is in me and if you offend me

I'm liftin' you ten feet (liftin' you ten feet) . . . in
the air
I don't care who was there and who saw me just jaw
you
Go call you a lawyer, file you a lawsuit
I'll smile in the courtroom and buy you a wardrobe
I'm tired of all you (of
all you) . . .
I don't mean to be mean but that's all I can be is
just me

CHORUS:
AND I AM WHATEVER YOU SAY I AM
IF I WASN'T, THEN WHY WOULD I SAY I AM?
IN THE PAPER, THE NEWS, EVERY DAY I AM
RADIO WON'T EVEN PLAY MY JAM
'CAUSE I AM WHATEVER YOU SAY I AM
IF I WASN'T, THEN WHY WOULD I SAY I AM?
IN THE PAPER, THE NEWS, EVERY DAY I AM
I DON'T KNOW, IT'S JUST THE WAY I AM

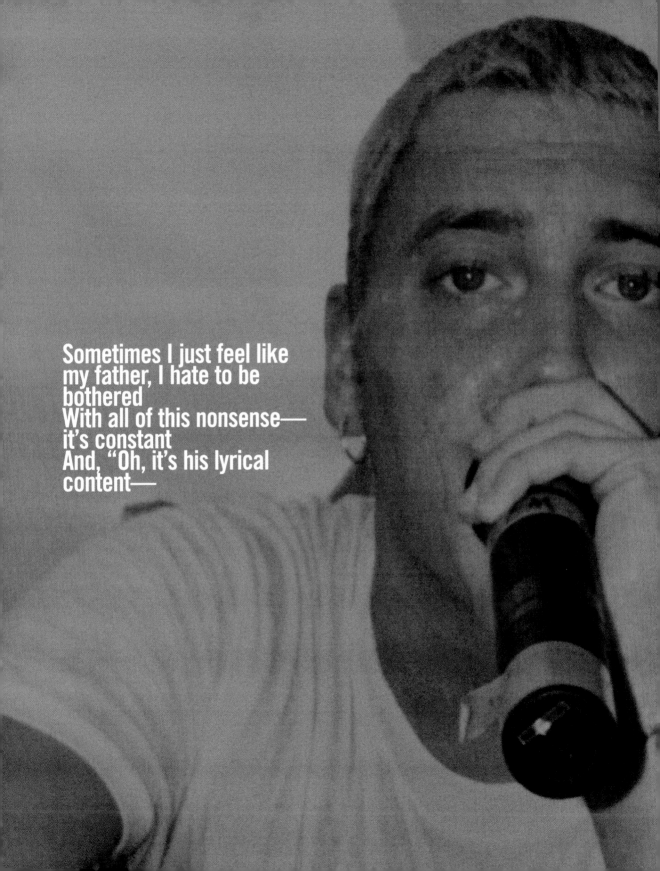

Sometimes I just feel like
my father, I hate to be
bothered
With all of this nonsense—
it's constant
And, "Oh, it's his lyrical
content—

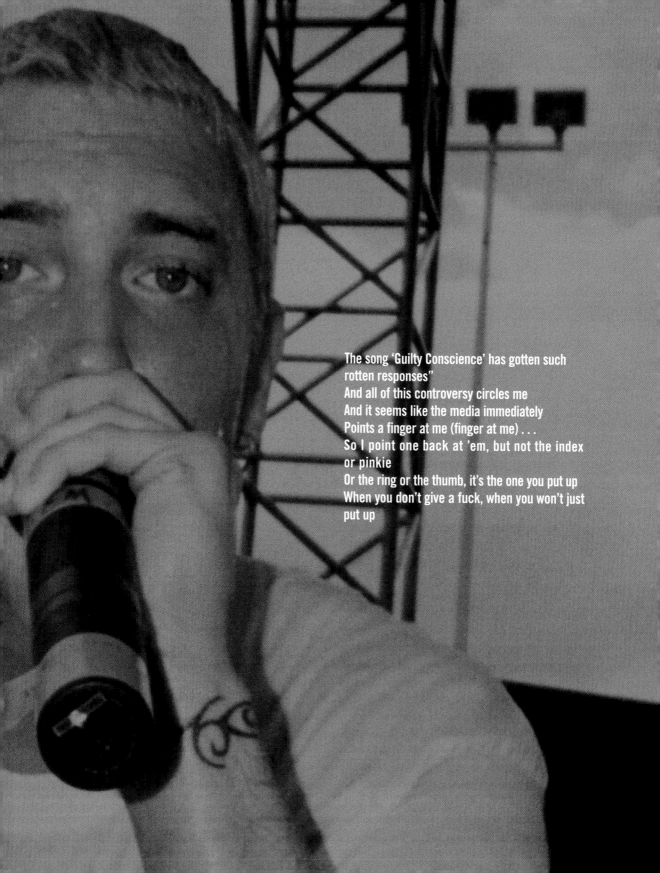

The song 'Guilty Conscience' has gotten such rotten responses"
And all of this controversy circles me
And it seems like the media immediately
Points a finger at me (finger at me) . . .
So I point one back at 'em, but not the index or pinkie
Or the ring or the thumb, it's the one you put up
When you don't give a fuck, when you won't just put up

With the bullshit they pull, 'cause they full of shit too

When a dude's gettin' bullied and shoots up his school

And they blame it on Marilyn (on Marilyn) . . . and the heroin

Where were the parents at? And look where it's at

Middle America, now it's a tragedy

Now it's so sad to see, an upper-class city

Havin' this happenin' (this happenin') . . .

Then attack Eminem 'cause I rap this way (rap this way) . . .

But I'm glad 'cause they feed me the fuel that I need for the fire

To burn and it's burnin' and I have returned

CHORUS

I'm so sick and tired of bein' admired

That I wish that I would just die or get fired

And dropped from my label

let's stop with the fables I'm not gonna be able to top a "My Name Is . . ."

And pigeonholed into some poppy sensation

To cop me rotation at rock-'n'-roll stations

And I just do not got the patience (got the patience) . . . To deal with these cocky caucasians

Who think I'm some wigger who just tries to be black

'Cuz I talk with an accent

And grab on my balls, so they always keep askin'

The same fuckin' questions (fuckin' questions) . . .

What school did I go to, what 'hood I grew up in

The why, the who, what, when, the where, and the how

Till I'm grabbin' my hair and I'm tearin' it out

'Cuz they drivin' me crazy (drivin' me crazy) . . .

I can't take it

I'm racin', I'm pacin', I stand then I sit

And I'm thankful for every fan that I get

But I can't take a SHIT in the bathroom Without someone standin' by it

No, I won't sign your autograph

You can call me an asshole—I'm glad

CHORUS

KILL YOU

What happened with "Kill You" was I came off the European tour in October of '99 and I called Dre and I told him that I needed some new tracks. He just happened to be going through some when I called. I remember him sayin', "I ain't really got no new tracks, but I'm trying to work on some new shit today." Meanwhile, there was a track playing in the background. I asked, "What's that?" He responded, "What's what? You mean this?" and he puts the phone to the speaker and it was the "Kill You" beat. I told him, "Send me that shit." He was really surprised. "You want this? This is some little shit we fuckin' with." I said, "Whatever, send me that. I . . . will . . . kill . . . that . . . track." He sent it to me the next day and I wrote the song. I recorded it weeks later when I started recording the *Marshall Mathers* album. The first thing I came up with was the hook: "You don't . . . wanna fuck with Shady . . . 'cause Shady . . . will fuckin' kill you." I wanted to start the album with that song because everybody in the press was like "What's he gonna rap about? He's not miserable anymore. He can't rap about being broke no more, he can't rhyme about his pain and his misery 'cause he's got money." That's why I started it up with that line "They said I can't rap about being broke no more, they ain't say I can't rap about coke no more." That right there gives you an idea of what the album's all about. The song is ridiculous. The whole hook is basically bashing women. Like, "I'll kill you even if you're a fuckin' girl." I kill bitches, I kill anybody, then at the end of the song I say, "I'm just kidding, ladies. You know I love you." It's kind of like you could say whatever you want as long as you say you're joking at the end. Which is cool 'cause that's what I do. It's funny 'cause people think that song is about my mother, all because of the first couple of lines. When I say, "When I was just a little baby boy," and when I say, "Oh now he's raping his own mother." After that the references just stop. The whole idea of this song was to say some of the most fucked-up shit. Just to let people know that I'm back. That I didn't lose it. That I wasn't compromising nothing and I didn't change. If anything . . . I got worse.

When I just a little baby boy,
My momma used to tell me these crazy things
She used to tell me my daddy was an evil man,
She used to tell me he hated me
But then I got a little bit older
And I realized she was the crazy one
But there was nothin' I could do or say to try to change it
'Cause that's just the way she was

They said I can't rap about bein' broke no more
They ain't say I can't rap about coke no more
(AHHH!) Slut, you think I won't choke no whore
Till the vocal cords don't work in her throat no more?!
(AHHH!) These motherfuckers are thinkin' I'm playin'
Thinkin' I'm sayin' the shit 'cause
I'm thinkin' it just to be sayin' it
(AHHH!) Put your hands down, bitch, I ain't gon' shoot you
I'ma pull YOU to this bullet, and put it through you
(AHHH!) Shut up, slut, you're causin' too much chaos
Just bend over and take it like a slut, okay, Ma?
"Oh, now he's raping his own mother, abusing a whore
Snorting coke, and we gave him the *Rolling Stone* cover?"
You goddamn right, BITCH, and now it's too late
I'm triple platinum and tragedies happened in two states
I invented violence, you vile venomous volatile vicious
Vain Vicadin, vrinnn Vrinnn, VRINNN! [chainsaw revs up]

Texas Chainsaw, left his brains all
Danglin' from his neck, while his head barely hangs on
Blood, guts, guns, cuts
Knives, lives, wives, nuns, sluts

CHORUS:
BITCH, I'MA KILL YOU! YOU DON'T WANNA FUCK WITH ME
GIRLS NEITHER—YOU AIN'T NUTTIN' BUT A SLUT TO ME
BITCH, I'MA KILL YOU! YOU AIN'T GOT THE BALLS TO BEEF
WE AIN'T GON' NEVER STOP BEEFIN' I DON'T SQUASH THE BEEF
YOU BETTER KILL ME! I'MA BE ANOTHER RAPPER DEAD
FOR POPPIN' OFF AT THE MOUTH WITH SHIT I SHOULDN'TA SAID
BUT WHEN THEY KILL ME—I'M BRINGIN' THE WORLD WITH ME
BITCHES TOO! YOU AIN'T NUTTIN' BUT A GIRL TO ME
. . . I SAID YOU DON'T WANNA FUCK WITH SHADY ('CAUSE WHY?)
'CAUSE SHADY WILL FUCKIN' KILL YOU (AH-HAHA)
I SAID YOU DON'T WANNA FUCK WITH SHADY (WHY?)
'CAUSE SHADY WILL FUCKIN' KILL YOU . . .

Bitch, I'ma kill you! Like a murder weapon, I'ma conceal you
In a closet with mildew, sheets, pillows and film you
Fuck with me, I been through hell, shut the hell up!
I'm tryin' to develop these pictures of the Devil to sell 'em
I ain't "acid rap," but I rap on acid
Got a new blowup doll and just had a strap-on added
WHOOPS! Is that a subliminal hint? NO!
Just criminal intent to sodomize women again
Eminem offend? NO!
Eminem will insult
And if you ever give in to him, you give him an impulse
To do it again, THEN, if he does it again
You'll probably end up jumpin' out of somethin' up on the tenth
(Ahhhhhhhh!) Bitch, I'ma kill you, I ain't done, this ain't the chorus
I ain't even drug you in the woods yet to paint the forest

A bloodstain is orange after you wash it three or four times
In a tub but that's normal, ain't it, Norman?
Serial killer hidin' murder material
In a cereal box on top of your stereo
Here we go again, we're out of our medicine
Out of our minds, and we want in yours, let us in

CHORUS (FIRST LINE STARTS "OR I'MA KILL YOU!")

Eh-heh, know why I say these things?
'Cause ladies' screams keep creepin' in Shady's dreams
And the way things seem, I shouldn't have to pay these shrinks
This eighty G's a week to say the same things TWEECE!
TWICE? Whatever, I hate these things
Fuck shots! I hope the weed'll outweigh these drinks
Motherfuckers want me to come on their radio shows
Just to argue with 'em 'cause their ratings stink?
FUCK THAT! I'll choke radio announcer to bouncer
From fat bitch to all seventy thousand pounds of her
From principal to the student body and counselor
From in school to before school to out of school
I don't even believe in breathin' I'm leavin' air in your lungs
Just to hear you keep screamin' for me to seep it
OKAY, I'M READY TO GO PLAY
I GOT THE MACHETE FROM O.J.
I'M READY TO MAKE EVERYONE'S THROATS ACHE
You faggots keep eggin' me on
Till I have you at knifepoint, then you beg me to stop?
SHUT UP! Give me your hands and feet
I said SHUT UP when I'm talkin' to you
YOU HEAR ME? ANSWER ME!

CHORUS (FIRST LINE STARTS "OR I'MA KILL YOU" NINTH LINE STARTS "BITCH, I'MA KILL YOU")

BLONDE 099

WHO KNEW

 "Who Knew" was the second song I recorded for the *Marshall Mathers* album. Dre was playin' a DAT and he was about to leave the studio. I wanted to hear some shit. So he played me some new shit and the "Who Knew" beat was one of the tracks on the DAT. I immediately thought "Oh my God, this is ridiculous." Dre left, but he said if I wanted to stay and record, then I should go ahead. See, what Dre does is he lays tracks to a DAT, but he won't complete them unless somebody wants 'em. He'll lay like ten or twenty down, and whoever likes 'em, they gotta rhyme to the track. Then he'll come in and re-do it the right way. So since he didn't have the beat laid down yet, I just rapped to the DAT. I had just come back from Amsterdam when I wrote that song. I had the hook, I had the verse, I had everything and it just mixed so perfectly with Dre's beat. So I said, "Fuck it" and recorded it that night. The next day he heard it and said, "Damn, you brought that shit to life. Let's get it in and knock it out." The whole idea behind this song was to try to make critics feel stupid. I think I countered everything that was said about me last year with *The Marshall Mathers LP*. Just like my next album will counter everything the critics said this year as far as gay bashing and all that shit goes. I just tried to make them look stupid and let them know not to take every fucking thing I say literally.

I never knew I . . .
I never knew I . . .
Mic check one-two
I never knew I . . .
Who woulda knew?
I never knew I . . .
Who'da known?
I never knew I . . .
Fuck would've thought
I never knew I . . .
Motherfucker comes out
I never knew I . . .
and sells a couple of million records
I never knew I . . .
And these motherfuckers hit the ceiling
I never knew I . . .

I don't do black music, I don't do white music
I make fight music, for high school kids
I put lives at risk when I drive like this [tires screech]
I put wives at risk with a knife like this (AHHH!!)
Shit, you probably think I'm in your tape deck now
I'm in the backseat of your truck,
with duct tape stretched out
Ducked the fuck way down, waitin' to straight jump out
Put it over your mouth,
and grab you by the face, what now?
Oh—you want me to watch my mouth, how?
Take my fuckin' eyeballs out, and turn 'em around?
Look—I'll burn your fuckin' house down, circle around
And hit the hydrant, so you can't put your burning furniture out
(Oh my God! Oh my God!) I'm sorry, there must be a mix-up
You want me to fix up lyrics while the president gets his
dick sucked?
Fuck that, take drugs, rape sluts
Make fun of gay clubs, men who wear makeup

Get aware, wake up, get a sense of humor
Quit tryin' to censor music, this is for your kid's amusement
(The kids!) But don't blame me when li'l Eric jumps off of the terrace
You shoulda been watchin' him—apparently you ain't parents

CHORUS:
'CAUSE I NEVER KNEW I, KNEW I WOULD GET THIS BIG
I NEVER KNEW I, KNEW I'D AFFECT THIS KID
I NEVER KNEW I'D GET HIM TO SLIT HIS WRIST
I NEVER KNEW I'D GET HIM TO HIT THIS BITCH
I NEVER KNEW I, KNEW I WOULD GET THIS BIG
I NEVER KNEW I, KNEW I'D AFFECT THIS KID
I NEVER KNEW I'D GET HIM TO SLIT HIS WRIST
I NEVER KNEW I'D GET HIM TO HIT THIS BITCH

So who's bringin' the guns in this country? (Hmm?)
I couldn't sneak a plastic pellet gun through customs over in London
And last week, I seen a Schwarzenegger movie
Where he's shootin' all sorts of these motherfuckers with a Uzi
I see these three little kids, up in the front row,
Screamin' "Go," with their seventeen-year-old uncle
I'm like, "Guidance—ain't they got the same moms and dads
Who got mad when I asked if they liked violence?"
And told me that my tape taught 'em to swear
What about the makeup you allow your twelve-year-old daughter to wear?
(Hmm?) So tell me that your son doesn't know any cusswords
When his bus driver's screamin' at him, fuckin' him up worse
("Go sit the fuck down, you little fuckin' prick!")
And *fuck* was the first word I ever learned
Up in the third grade, flippin' the gym teacher the bird (Look!)
So read up about how I used to get beat up
Peed on, be on free lunch, and change school every three months
My life's like kinda what my wife's like (what?)
Fucked up after I beat her

fuckin' ass every night, Ike

So how much easier would life be
If nineteen million motherfuckers grew to be just like me?

CHORUS

I never knew I . . . knew I'd . . .
Have a new house or a new car
A couple years ago I was more poorer than you are

I don't got that bad of a mouth, do I?

Fuck shit ass bitch cunt, shooby-de-doo-wop (what?)
Skibbedy-be-bop, a-Christopher Reeve
Sonny Bono, skis horses and hittin' some trees (HEY!)

How many retards'll listen to me
And run up in the school shootin' when they're pissed at a
Teach-er, her, him, is it you, is it them?

"Wasn't me, Slim Shady said to do it again!"
Damn! How much damage can you do with a pen?
Man, I'm just as fucked up as you woulda been
If you woulda been in my shoes, who woulda thought
Slim Shady would be somethin' that you woulda bought
That woulda made you get a gun and shoot at a cop
I just said it—I ain't know if you'd do it or not

CHORUS

How the fuck was I supposed to know?

THE REAL SL

 Okay, so they made me do the single. Thing was, I had that hook for a minute, but I was nervous about doing anything with it. I didn't even bring it to Dre. He didn't know I had it in store, stockpiled with a bunch of other hooks. See, I write the hooks a lot of times before I write the actual rhyme. So I had this hook, but I asked myself, "Will this work?" It just needed the right beat. Man, we went into the studio about four times tryin' to come up with one. We did about four or five different tracks and still nothing was working. Finally, me and Dre was in the studio and we had just about given up. I was laid out on the couch, exhausted, and Dre was about to leave the room. I was tellin' the bass player and keyboard player to play something till I liked it. So they kept fuckin' around, fuckin' around, and fuckin' around till Tommy (one of Dre's keyboard players) played the first few notes of "The Real Slim Shady" and I jumped up and said, "What was that?" I then asked him to do something different with it. Make it go up, and then down. He did a couple of different things

with it until I was like "Right there." I then ran and got Dre to come listen to it. They added drums. Now, this all happened on a Friday. We had a meeting on Saturday with the label and they asked, "Well, did you come up with anything?" I played them "The Way I Am" and they said, "It's a great song. It's just not the first song." Originally, they were talkin' about "Criminal" being the single, but I told them to let me take this shit ("The Real Slim Shady" instrumental) over the weekend and I'd have the rhyme written by Monday. Then we'd see if it worked. If it didn't, then fuck it. Right around this time was when Will Smith was dissin' gangsta rap and Christina Aguilera was talkin' shit about me on MTV, putting me on blast about being married during a time when I wasn't ready for the public to know that about me yet. So I waited just long enough to get new subject matter to get into. Now I had something to talk about. I came in on Monday, recorded it, and was done. Interscope, obviously, was satisfied. That situation made me

May I have your attention please?
May I have your attention please?
Will the real Slim Shady please stand up?
I repeat, will the real Slim Shady please stand up?
We're gonna have a problem here . . .

Y'all act like you never seen a white person before
Jaws all on the floor like Pam, like Tommy just
burst in the door
And started whoopin' her ass worse than before
They first were divorced
throwin' her over furniture (Ahh!)

It's the return of the . . . "Ah, wait, no wait,
you're kidding,
He didn't just say what I think he did, did he?"
And Dr. Dre said . . . nothing, you idiots!
Dr. Dre's dead, he's locked in my basement!
(Ha-ha!)
Feminist women love Eminem
[vocal turntable: chigga chigga chigga]
"Slim Shady, I'm sick of him
Look at him, walkin' around grabbin' his you-
know-what
Flippin' the you-know-who," "Yeah, but he's so

cute though!"
Yeah, I probably got a couple of screws up in my head loose
But no worse than what's goin' on in your parents' bedrooms
Sometimes, I wanna get on TV and just let loose, but can't
But it's cool for Tom Green to hump a dead moose
"My bum is on your lips, my bum is on your lips"
And if I'm lucky, you might just give it a little kiss
And that's the message that we deliver to little kids
And expect them not to know what a woman's

clitoris is
Of course they gonna know what intercourse is
By the time they hit fourth grade
They got the Discovery Channel, don't they?
"We ain't nothing but mammals . . ." Well, some of us cannibals
Who cut other people open like cantaloupes [SLURP]
But if we can hump dead animals and antelopes
Then there's no reason that a man and another man can't elope [EWWW!]
But if you feel like I feel, I got the antidote

Women wave your panty hose, sing the chorus and it goes

CHORUS (REPEAT 2X):
I'M SLIM SHADY, YES I'M THE REAL SHADY
ALL YOU OTHER SLIM SHADYS ARE JUST IMITATING
SO WON'T THE REAL SLIM SHADY PLEASE STAND UP
PLEASE STAND UP, PLEASE STAND UP?

Will Smith don't gotta cuss in his raps to sell records
Well, I do, so fuck him and fuck you too!
You think I give a damn about a Grammy?
Half of you critics can't even stomach me, let alone stand me
"But Slim, what if you win, wouldn't it be weird?"
Why? So you guys could just lie to get me here?
So you can sit me here next to Britney Spears?
Shit, Christina Aguilera better switch me chairs
So I can sit next to Carson Daly and Fred Durst
And hear 'em argue over who she gave head to first
You little bitch, put me on blast on MTV
"Yeah, he's cute, but I think he's married to Kim, hee-hee!"

I should download her audio on MP3
And show the whole world how you gave Eminem VD
(AHHH!)
I'm sick of you little girl and boy groups, all you do is
annoy me
So I have been sent here to destroy you [bzzzt]
And there's a million of us just like me
Who cuss like me, who just don't give a fuck like me
Who dress like me, walk, talk, and act like me
And just might be the next best thing but not quite me!

I'm like a head trip to listen to, 'cause I'm only givin' you
Things you joke about with your friends inside your living room
The only difference is I got the balls to say it in front of y'all
And I don't gotta be false or sugarcoat it at all
I just get on the mic and spit it
And whether you like to admit it [ERR] I just shit it
Better than ninety percent of you rappers out can
Then you wonder how can kids eat up these albums like Valiums
It's funny, 'cause at the rate I'm goin' when I'm thirty
I'll be the only person in the nursin' home flirting
Pinchin' nurses' asses when I'm jackin' off with Jergens
And I'm jerkin' but this whole bag of Viagra isn't workin'
And every single person is a Slim Shady lurkin'
He could be workin' at Burger King
Spittin' on your onion rings [HACH]
Or in the parkin' lot, circling
Screaming "I don't give a fuck!"
With his windows down and his system up
So, will the real Shady please stand up?
And put one of those fingers on each hand up?
And be proud to be outta your mind and outta control
And one more time, loud as you can, how does it go?

CHORUS 2X

Ha-ha
Guess there's a Slim Shady in all of us
Fuck it, let's all stand up

BLONDE 111

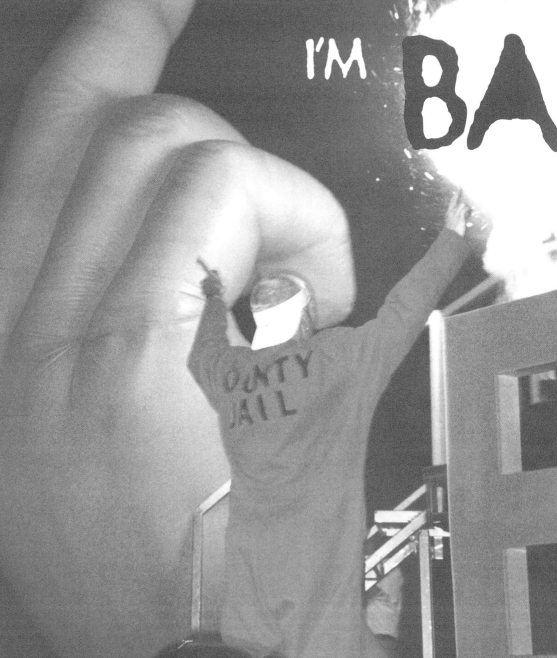

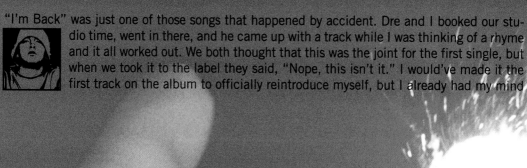
"I'm Back" was just one of those songs that happened by accident. Dre and I booked our studio time, went in there, and he came up with a track while I was thinking of a rhyme and it all worked out. We both thought that this was the joint for the first single, but when we took it to the label they said, "Nope, this isn't it." I would've made it the first track on the album to officially reintroduce myself, but I already had my mind

I'M BA

set on "Kill You." Spontaneous sessions like this one make me appreciate the chemistry that has grown between the Doc and me. It's one thing to strain ourselves for a good song. But when his vibe and mine naturally connect on a quick song that's just as good, the results reassure me and make me feel that I'm not just a rapper on one of his beats, but I'm also a partner in the music-making process.

CK

CHORUS (REPEAT 4X):
THAT'S WHY THEY CALL ME SLIM SHADY (I'M BACK)
I'M BACK (I'M BACK) [SLIM SHADY!] I'M BACK

I murder a rhyme one word at a time
You never heard of a mind as perverted as mine
You better get rid of that nine, it ain't gonna help
What good's it gonna do against a man that strangles himself?

I'm waitin' for hell like hell shit I'm anxious as hell
Manson, you're safe in that cell, be thankful it's jail
I used to be my mommy's little angel at twelve
At thirteen I was puttin' shells in a gauge on the shelf
I used to get punked and bullied on my block
Till I cut a kitten's head off and stuck it in this kid's mailbox ("Mom! MOM!")
I used to give a—fuck, now I could give a fuck less
What do I think of success? It sucks, too much press, stress,
Too much cess, depressed, too upset
It's just too much mess, I guess
I must just blew up quick (yes)
Grew up quick (no) was raised right
Whatever you say's wrong, whatever I say's right
You think of my name now whenever you say, "Hi"
Became a commodity because I'm W-H-I-T-E,
'cause MTV was so friendly to me
Can't wait till Kim sees me
Now is it worth it? Look at my life, how is it perfect?
Read my lips, bitch, what, my mouth isn't workin?
You hear this finger? Oh it's upside down
Here, let me turn this motherfucker up right now

CHORUS

I take each individual degenerate's head and reach into it
Just to see if he's influenced by me if he listens to music
And if he feeds into this shit he's an innocent victim
And becomes a puppet on the string of my tennis shoe [vocal scratches]
My name is Slim Shady
I been crazy way before radio didn't play me
The sensational [vocal scratch "Back is the incredible!"]
With Ken Kaniff, who just finds the men edible
It's Ken Kaniff on the Internet
Tryin' to lure your kids with him, into bed
It's a sick world we live in these days
"Slim, for Pete's sakes, put down Christopher Reeve's legs!"
Geez, you guys are so sensitive
"Slim, it's a touchy subject, try and just don't mention it"
Mind with no sense in it, fried schizophrenic
Whose eyes get so squinted, I'm blind from smokin 'em
With my windows tinted, with nine limos rented

Doin' lines of coke in 'em, with a bunch of guys hoppin' out
All high and indo scented [inhales, exhales]
And that's where I get my name from, that's why they call me

I take seven kids from Columbine, stand 'em all in line
Add an AK-47, a revolver, a nine
A Mack-11 and it oughta solve the problem of mine
And that's a whole school of bullies shot up all at one time
'Cause (I'mmmm) Shady, they call me as crazy
As the world was over this whole Y2K thing
And by the way, N'Sync, why do they sing?
Am I the only one who realizes they stink?
Should I dye my hair pink and care what y'all think?
Lip-synch and buy a bigger size of earrings?
It's why I tend to block out when I hear things
'Cause all these fans screamin' is makin' my ears ring (AHHHH!!!)
So I just throw up a middle finger and let it linger
Longer than the rumor that I was stickin' it to Christina
'Cause if I ever stuck it to any singer in showbiz
It'd be Jennifer Lopez, and Puffy, you know this!
I'm sorry, Puff, but I don't give a fuck if this chick was my own mother
I'd still fuck her with no rubber and cum inside her
And have a son and a new brother at the same time
And just say that it ain't mine, what's my name?

CHORUS

[vocal scratching]
Guess who's b-back, back
Gue-gue-guess who's back (Hi Mom!)
[scratch] Guess who's back
[scratch] Gue [scratch] guess who's back
D-12 [scratch] Guess who's back
Gue, gue-gue-gue, guess who's back
Dr. Dre [scratch] Guess who's back
Back back [scratch] back
[scratch]
Slim Shady, 2001
I'm blew out from this blunt [sighs] fuck

GREG
FREESTYLE

I kicked this during my first big radio appearance. It was on the *Sway and Tech Show* in L.A. It was the day after the Rap Olympics. That was actually one of the first few rhymes that I wrote as Slim Shady. Yeah, it's one to get you mad. This is another one of those verses that I write to throw out there if somebody says, "Yo, let me hear you spit." If somebody really wants to hear you rap, they don't want to hear you freestyle like "Yo my house, I got a mouse with a blouse." Nobody cares about that shit. If you really want to show someone what you're about, you have a written rhyme ready, a rhyme that you fuckin' wrote and took your time with and thought out, and spit that for them. People used to ask me who Greg was. Honestly, I don't know. I just decided to start the rhyme off with "I met a retarded kid named Greg with a wooden leg / snatched it off and beat him over his fuckin' head wit' the peg." If there is a kid named Greg with a wooden leg reading this, it was only a joke.

Met a retarded kid named Greg with a wooden leg
Snatched it off and beat him over the fucking head wit' the peg

Go to bed with a keg, wake up with a 40
Mixed up with Alka-Seltzer and Formula 44D
Fuck an acid tab I strapped the whole sheet to my forehead
Wait until it absorbed in and fell to the floor dead
No more said, case closed, end of discussion
I'm blowin' up like spontaneous human combustion
Leaving you in the aftermath of holocaust and traumas
Cross the bombers
We blowin' up your house, killing your parents
And coming back to get your foster mommas
And I'm as good at keeping a promise as Nostradamus
'Cause I ain't making no more threats
I'm doing drive-bys in tinted Corvettes on Vietnam War vets
I'm more or less sick in the head
Maybe more 'cause I smoked crack
Today, yesterday, and the day before
Saboteur, walk the block with a Labrador
Strap with more coral for war than El Salvador
Foul style galore
Verbal cow manure
Coming together like the eyebrow on Al B. Sure

It's only fair to warn I was born with a set of horns

And metaphors attached to my damn umbilical cord

Warlord of rap that'll bush you with a two-by-four board

And smashed into your Honda Accord

With a four-door Ford

But I'm more towards droppin' an a cappella

That's choppin' a fella into mozzarella

Worse than a hellacopta propella

Got you locked in the cella'

With your skeleton showing

Developing anorexia

While I'm standin' next to ya

Eating a full-course meal watching you starve to death

With an IV in your veins

Feeding you liquid Darvocet

Pumping you full of drugs

Pull the plugs

On the gunshot victims full of bullet slugs

Who were picked up in an ambulance

And driven

To Receiving with the asses ripped outta they pants

And given

A less than 20 percent chance

Of living

Have a possible placement

As a hospital patient

Storing the dead bodies in Grandma's little basement

Dr. Kevorkian has arrived

To perform an autopsy on you while you scream "I'M STILL ALIVE!"

Driving a rusty scalpel in through the top of your scalp

And pulling your Adam's apple out through your mouth

Better call the fire department

I've hired an arson

To set fire to carpet

And burn up your entire apartment

I'm a liar that starts shit

Got your bitch wrapped around my dick

So tight you need a crowbar to pry her apart wit'

ANY MAN

Hi!
Original Bad Boy on the case, cover your face
Came in the place, blowed, and sprayed Puffy with Mase
I laced the weed with insect repellent, better check to smell it
Eminem starts with *E*, better check to spell it
With a capital, somebody grab me a Snapple
I got an aspirin capsule trapped in my Adam's apple
Somebody dropped me on my head, and I was sure
That my mother did it, but the bitch won't admit it was her
I slit her stomach open with a scalpel when she was six months
And said, "I'm ready now, bitch—ain't you feelin' these kicks, cunt?"

The world ain't ready for me yet, I can tell
I'll probably have a cell next to the furnace in hell

I'm sicker than sperm cells with syphilis germs
And I'm hotter than my dick is, when I piss and it burns
I kick you in the tummy until you sick to your stomach
And vomit so much blood that your clothes stick to you from it (Yuck!)
Hit you in the head with a brick till you plummet
If y'all don't like me, you can suck my dick till you numb it
And all that gibberish you was spittin', you need to kill it
'Cause your style is like dyin' in my sleep, I don't feel it

CHORUS:
'CAUSE ANY MAN WHO WOULD JUMP IN FRONT OF A MINIVAN
FOR TWENTY GRAND AND A BOTTLE OF PAIN PILLS AND A MINI THIN
IS FUCKIN' CRAZY—YOU HEAR ME? HA?
IS FUCKIN' CRAZY—HELLO, HI!
'CAUSE ANY MAN WHO WOULD JUMP IN FRONT OF A MINIVAN
FOR TWENTY GRAND AND A BOTTLE OF PAIN PILLS AND A MINI THIN
IS FUCKIN' CRAZY—DO YOU HEAR ME?
IS FUCKIN' CRAZY

I'm ice grillin' you, starin' you down with a gremlin grin
I'm Eminem, you're a fag in a women's gym
I'm Slim, the Shady is really a fake alias
To save me with in case I get chased by space aliens
A brainiac, with a cranium packed full of more uranium
Than a maniac Saudi Arabian
A highly combustible head, spazmatic
Strapped to a Craftmatic adjustable bed
Laid up in the hospital in critical condition
I flatlined; jumped up and ran from the mortician
High speed, IV full of Thai weed
Lookin' Chinese, with my knees stuck together
like Siamese Twins, joined at the groin like lesbians
Uhh, pins and needles, hypodermic needles and pins
I hope God forgives me for my sins—it probably all depends
On if I keep on killin' my girlfriends

CHORUS:
'CAUSE ANY MAN WHO WOULD JUMP IN FRONT
OF A MINIVAN
FOR TWENTY GRAND AND A BOTTLE OF PAIN
PILLS AND A MINI THIN
IS FUCKIN' CRAZY—YOU HEAR ME? HA?
IS FUCKIN' CRAZY—LISTEN!!
'CAUSE ANY MAN WHO WOULD JUMP IN FRONT
OF A MINIVAN
FOR TWENTY GRAND AND A BOTTLE OF PAIN
PILLS AND A MINI THIN
IS FUCKIN' CRAZY—YOU HEAR ME?
IS FUCKIN' CRAZY

Last night I OD'd on rush, mushrooms, and dust
And got rushed to the hospital to get my system flushed
(Shucks!) I'm an alcoholic and that's all I can say
I call in to work, 'cause all I do is frolic and play
I swallow grenades, and take about a bottle a day
Of Tylenol 3, and talk about how violent I'll be
(RRARRRRH)
Give me eleven Excedrin, my head'll spin
Medicine'll get me revvin' like a 747 jet engine
Scratched my balls till I shredded skin
"Doctor, check this rash, look how red it's been"
"It's probably AIDS!" Forget it then
I strike a still pose and hit you with some ill flows
That don't even make sense, like dykes usin' dildos
So reach in your billfolds, for ten duckets
And pick up this Slim Shady shit that's on Rawkus
Somethin' somethin' somethin', somethin' I get weeded
My daughter scribbled over that rhyme, I couldn't read it
Damn!

MURDER MUR

CHORUS (REPEAT 4X):
IT'S MURDER SHE WROTE
(IT'S MURDER SHE WROTE)
IT WASN'T NUTTIN' FOR HER TO BE SMOKED
(FOR HER TO BE SMOKED)

Left the keys in the van, with a Gat in each hand
Went up in Eastland and shot a policeman
Fuck a peace plan, if a citizen bystands
The shit is in my hands, here's yo' lifespan
And for what yo' life's worth, this money is twice than
Grab a couple grand and lay up in Iceland
See, I'm a nice man but money turned me to Satan
I'm thirsty for this green so bad I'm dehydratin'
Hurry up with the cash, bitch, I got a ride waitin'
Shot a man twice in the back when he tried skatin'
I want the whole pie, I won't be denied Nathan
Maybe I need my head inside straightened
Brain contemplatin', clean out the register
Dip before somebody catches ya
Or gets a description and sketches ya
And connects you as the prime suspect
But I ain't set to flee the scene of the crime

just yet
'Cause I got a daughter to feed
And $200 ain't enough to water the seed
The best thing would be for me to leave Taco Bell and hit up Chess King
And have the lady at the desk bring
Money from the safe in the back, stepped in wavin' the Mac
Cooperate, and we can operate, and save an attack
This bitch tried escapin' the jack
Grabbed her by the throat, it's murder she wrote
You barely heard a word as she choked
It wasn't nuttin' for her to be smoked
But I slammed her on her back till her vertebrae broke
Just then the pigs bust in yellin' "Freeze"
But I'm already wanted for sellin' keys
And bunch of other felonies from A to Z like spellin' bees
So before I dropped to the ground and fell on knees
I bust shots, they bust back
Hit me square in the chest, wasn't wearin' a vest

DER (REMIX)

Left the house, pullin' out the drive backin' out
Blew the back end out this lady's Jag, started blackin' out
Pulled the Mac-10 out, stuck it in her face
Shut your yackin' mouth, 'fore I blow the brain from out the back ya scalp
Drug her by her hair, smacked her up
Thinkin' fuck it, mug her while you're there, jacked her up
Stole her car, made a profit
Grabbed the tape from out the deck and loft it out the window
Like the girl in *Set It Off* did
Jetted off kid, stole the whip, now I'm a criminal
Drove it through somebody's yard, dove into they swimmin' pool
Climbed out and collapsed on the patio
I made it out alive but I'm injured badly though

Parents screamin', "Johnny, go in and call the police Tell 'em there's a crazy man disturbing all of the peace!"

Tried to stall him at least long enough to let me leap up
Run in they crib and at least leave with some little cheap stuff
Actin' like they never seen nobody hit a lick before
Smashed the window, grabbed the Nintendo 64

When they sell out in stores the price triples

I ran up the block jumpin' kids on tricycles And collided with an eighty-year-old lady with groceries There goes cheese, eggs, milk, and Post Toasties

Stood up and started to see stars
So many siren sounds, it seemed like a thousand police cars
Barely escaped, must a been some dumb luck
Jumped up and climbed the back of a movin' dump truck
But I think somebody seen me maybe
Plus I lost the damn Nintendo and I musta dropped the Beanie Baby
Fuck it, I give up, I'm surrounded in blue suits
Came out with a white flag hollerin' "TRUCE TRUCE"
And surrendered my weapon to cops
Wasn't me! It was the gangster rap and the peppermint schnapps

CHORUS
CHORUS (REPEATS AGAIN TO FADE)

BAD INFLUENCE

The hook to "Bad Influence" wasn't originally a hook, but part of an ill rhyme that I had written. It's so funny, 'cause I really shot myself in the foot during the time I was writing this. I wrote a song two years ago that I wanted to record with the rhyme *"People say that I'm a bad influence."* I just wrote the rhyme but never really practiced it. I was gonna practice saying it my head, but the day after I wrote it, I had lost the sheet of paper that I had written the shit on. Man, I tell you, there was so much dope shit that I lost on that piece of paper. Honestly, I think somebody stole it out of my apartment in Cali when I was out there. The only things I could remember from that song was "People say that I'm a bad influence / I say the world's already fucked, I'm just addin' to it" and "They say I'm sui-

cidal." Since those were the only lines I could recall, I used it as a hook. "Bad Influence" was one of the few tracks that FBT ever did without me being there. They were just fucking with the track and happened to have it. I said, "Yo, I gotta rhyme to it" and wrote the verses immediately . . . and that was it. I recorded it right after the "Kim" song. I was gonna use it for the next album and then for the *Celebrity Death Match Soundtrack*. The verses were meant to be thrown out there at college radio stations and shit like that. I call 'em dummy verses. Somebody says "Spit some shit," this is what I'm gonna spit if I don't feel like freestyling.

(JUST PULL THE PLUG!)
PEOPLE SAY THAT I'M A BAD INFLUENCE
I SAY THE WORLD'S ALREADY FUCKED, I'M JUST
ADDIN' TO IT
THEY SAY I'M SUICIDAL
TEENAGERS' NEWEST IDOL
C'MON, DO AS I DO
GO AHEAD GET MAD AND DO IT
[REPEAT ALL 2X]

Hand me an eighth
Beam me up and land me in space
I'ma sit on top of the world (I'm here)
And shit on Brandy and Mase
I'm more than ill
Scarier than a white journalist in a room with Lauryn Hill (ahhh)
Human horror film
But with a lot funnier plot
And people'll feel me 'cause
I'ma still be the mad rapper whether I got money or not (yup)
As long as I'm on pills, and I got plenty of pot
I'll be in a canoe paddlin' makin' fun of your yacht

But I would like an award
For the best rapper to get one mic in *The Source*

And a wardrobe I can afford
Otherwise I might get end up back striking at Ford
And you wonder what the fuck I need more Vicadin for
Everybody's pissin' me off; even the No Limit tank looks like
A middle finger sideways flippin' me off
No shit, I'm a grave danger to my health
Why else would I kill you and jump in a grave and bury myself?

(JUST PULL THE PLUG!)
PEOPLE SAY THAT I'M A BAD INFLUENCE
I SAY THE WORLD'S ALREADY FUCKED, I'M JUST ADDIN' TO IT
THEY SAY I'M SUICIDAL
TEENAGERS' NEWEST IDOL
C'MON, DO AS I DO
GO AHEAD GET MAD AND DO IT
(JUST LET IT GO!)
[REPEAT ALL 2X]

I'm the illest rapper to hold the cordless, patrolling corners
Looking for hookers to punch in the mouth with a roll of quarters
I'm meaner in action than Rosco beating James Todd Senior
Across the back with vacuum cleaner attachments (ouch ouch)
I grew up in the wild 'hood, as a hazardous youth
With a fucked-up childhood that I used as an excuse
And ain't shit changed, I kept the same mind state
Since the third time that I failed ninth grade
You probably think that I'm a negative person

Don't be so sure of it
I don't promote violence, I just encourage it (c'mon)
I laugh at the sight of death
As I fall down a cement flight of steps (ahhhh)
And land inside a bed of spiderwebs
So throw caution to the wind, you and a friend
Can jump off of a bridge, and if you live, do it again
Shit, why not? Blow your brain out
I'm blowing mine out
Fuck it, you only live once, you might as well die now

(JUST LET IT GO)
PEOPLE SAY THAT I'M A BAD INFLUENCE
I SAY THE WORLD'S ALREADY FUCKED, I'M JUST ADDIN' TO IT
THEY SAY I'M SUICIDAL
TEENAGERS' NEWEST IDOL
C'MON, DO AS I DO
GO AHEAD GET MAD AND DO IT
(JUST PULL THE PLUG!)
[REPEAT ALL 2X]

My laser disc will make you take a razor to your wrist
Make you satanistic
Make you take the pistol to your face
And place the clip and cock it back
And let it go until your brains are rippin' out your skull so bad
To sew you back would be a waste of stitches

I'm not a "Role Model," I don't wanna baby-sit kids
I got one little girl, and Hailie Jade is Shady's business

And Shady's just an alias I made to make you pissed off
Where the fuck were you when Gilbert's paid to make me dishwash
I make a couple statements and now look how crazy shit got
You made me get a bigger attitude than eighty Kim Scotts
And she almost got the same fate that Grady's bitch got
I knew that "Just the Two of Us" would make you hate me this much
And "Just the Two of Us"
That ain't got shit to do with us in our personal life

It's just words on a mic

So you can call me a punk, a pervert, or a chauvinist pig
But the funny shit is that I still go with the bitch

FUCK
THE PLANET
(FREESTYLE)

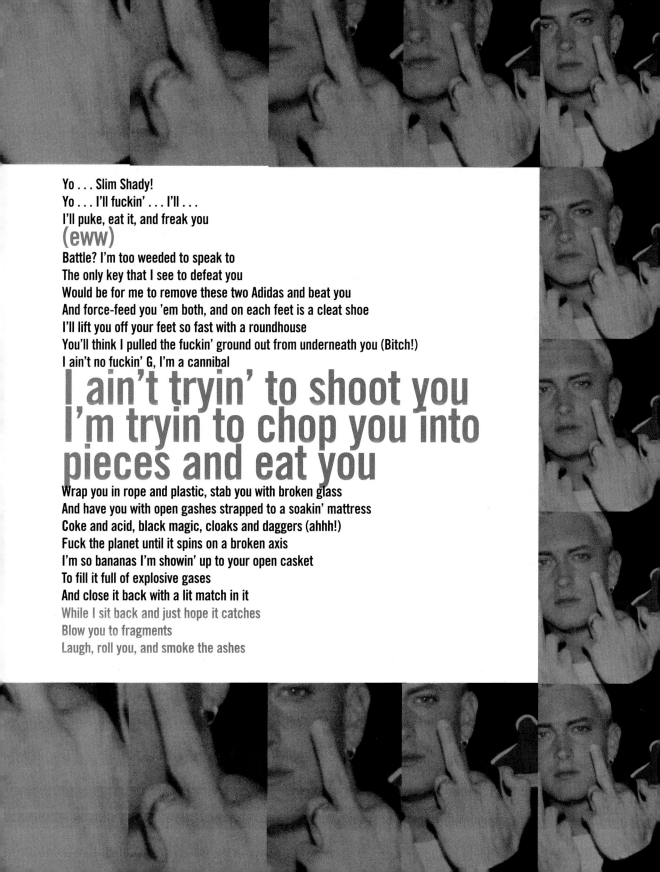

Yo . . . Slim Shady!
Yo . . . I'll fuckin' . . . I'll . . .
I'll puke, eat it, and freak you
(eww)
Battle? I'm too weeded to speak to
The only key that I see to defeat you
Would be for me to remove these two Adidas and beat you
And force-feed you 'em both, and on each feet is a cleat shoe
I'll lift you off your feet so fast with a roundhouse
You'll think I pulled the fuckin' ground out from underneath you (Bitch!)
I ain't no fuckin' G, I'm a cannibal

I ain't tryin' to shoot you I'm tryin to chop you into pieces and eat you

Wrap you in rope and plastic, stab you with broken glass
And have you with open gashes strapped to a soakin' mattress
Coke and acid, black magic, cloaks and daggers (ahhh!)
Fuck the planet until it spins on a broken axis
I'm so bananas I'm showin' up to your open casket
To fill it full of explosive gases
And close it back with a lit match in it
While I sit back and just hope it catches
Blow you to fragments
Laugh, roll you, and smoke the ashes

[Eminem verse only]

Nobody better test me, 'cause I don't wanna get messy
Especially when I step inside this bitch, dipped freshly
New Lugz, give the crew hugs, guzzle two mugs
Before I do drugs that make me throw up like flu bugs
True thugs, rugged unshaven messy scrubs
Grippin' 40-bottles like the fuckin' Pepsi clubs
Down a fifth, crack open a sixth
I'm on my seventh 8-ball, now I gotta take a piss
I'm hollerin' at these hos that got boyfriends
Who gives a fuck who they was
I'm always takin' someone else's girl like Cool J does

NO ONE'S

ANGRY

130

Me, Swift, Bizzare, Fuzz, and Proof were the illest emcees in Detroit. One time we found ourselves with access to a studio. So we decided to cut a song together. I was trying
to get a hold of Proof and couldn't find him. I called Bizzare and he said, "Yo,
get Swift on it," so we did. And then we wanted to get Fuzz on the track, 'cause
Fuzz was just ridiculous. Proof wasn't available for the song, and besides, he didn't
get along with Fuzz. DJ Head had the track, and we laid it down. Everybody came
to the studio and wrote their shit. Fuzz wrote his on the spot. Me, Bizzare, and Swift already

They probably don't be packin' anyways, do they, Fuzz?
We walked up, stomped they asses, and blew they buzz
Mics get sandblasted
Stab your abdomen with a handcrafted pocketknife and spill your antacid
Sprayed your motherfuckin' crib up when I ran past it
Fuckin' felon, headed to hell in a handbasket
Talkin' shit will get you, your girl, and your man blasted
Kidnapped and slapped in a van wrapped in Saran plastic
Get your damn ass kicked by these fantastic
Furious four motherfuckers
Flashin' in front of your face without the Grand Masters

Slim Shady, ain't nobody iller than me

ILLER

had ours done. Bizzare thought of the hook when he heard the beat. "No one iller than me." There was an energy that I'll never forget. Swift went into the booth and spit the first verse. Everybody was like "Iiiiill, iiiill." Then Bizzare went in and again, "Iiill, iiiill, iiiill." I spit my lines and everybody repeated "Iiill, iiiill, iiill, iiiill." Then Fuzz went and spit his shit in one take and he was just a blur of nonstop words. We were like "Oooohh fuck." It all went in a perfect order. Each verse was iller than the next. It was such a buildup song. That's the vibe we plan on capturing on D-12's debut album.

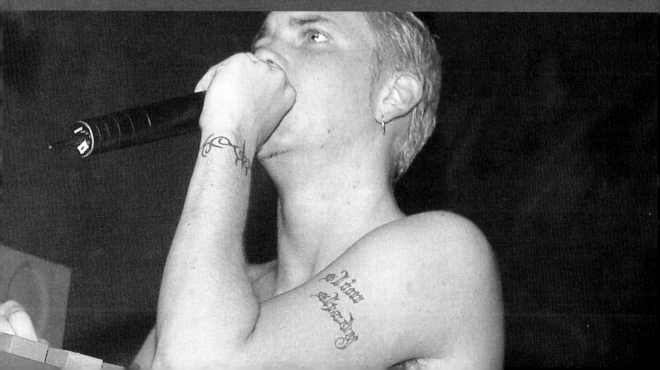

LowDOWN

Warning, this shit's gon' be rated R, restricted
You see this bullet hole in my neck? It's self-inflicted

Doctor slapped my momma, "Bitch, you got a sick kid" Arrested, molested myself and got convicted

Wearing visors, sunglasses, and disguises
'Cause my split personality is having an identity crisis
I'm Dr. Hyde and Mr. Jekyll, disrespectful
Hearing voices in my head while these whispers echo
"Murder Murder Redrum"
Brain size of a bread crumb
Which drug will I end up dead from
Inebriated, till my stress is alleviated
"How in the fuck can Eminem and Shady be related?"
Illiterate, illegitimate shit spitter
Bitch getter, hid in the bush like Margot Kidder
Jumped out (Ahhhh!) killed the bitch and did her
Use to let the baby-sitter suck my dick when I
was littler
Smoke a blunt while I'm titty-fuckin' Bette Midler
Sniper, waiting on your roof like the Fiddler
Y'all thought I was gonna rhyme with Riddler

Didn't ya? Bring your bitch, I wanna see if this dick
gon' fit in her

CHORUS:
I'M LOW DOWN AND I'M SHIFTY!
"AND IF YOU HEAR A MAN THAT SOUNDS LIKE
ME, SMACK HIM
AND ASK HIM WHERE THE FUCK DID HE GET HIS
DAMN RAPS FROM . . ."

I lace tunes that's out this world like space moons
With a bunch crazed loons that's missin' brains
like braze wounds
Nothing but idiots and misfits, dipshits
Doing whippits, passed out like sampler snippets
Where's the weed, I wanna tamper with it
I'ma let your grandpa hit it
Mix it up with cocaine so he can't forget it
Fuck it, maybe I'm a bum
But I was put on this earth to make your baby
mama cum
See what I'm on is way beyond the rum or any
alcoholic beverage
Losing all of my leverage
Went up inside the First National Bank broke, and
left rich
Walking biohazard causing wreckage
Smoked out like Eckridge
Dandruff making my neck itch

RTY

What the fuck? Gimme my check, bitch

You just lost your tip, there's a pubic hair in my breakfast

Got shit popping off like bottle cap tips
Get your cap peeled like the dead skin off your mama's chapped lips
Slap dips, support domestic violence
Beat your bitch's ass while your kids stare in silence
I'm just joking, is Dirty Dozen really dust smoking?
If all your shit's missing, then probably one of us broke in

CHORUS

My head's ringing, like it was spider sense tinglin'
Blitzin' like Green Bay did when they shitted on New England
I'm out the game, put the second string in
This brandy got me swinging

Bobbing back and forth like a penguin
Delinquent, toting microphones with broken English
Make your mama be like "Ohh! This is good! Who sing this?"
"Slim Shady, his tape is dope, I dug it
It's rugged, but he needs to quit talking all that drug shit."
It was predicted by a medic I'd grow to be an addicted diabetic
Living off liquid Triaminic
Pathetic, and I don't think this headache's ever vanishing
Panicking, I think I might have just took too much Anacin
Frozen Mannequin posin' stiffer than a statue
I think I'm dying, God is that you?
Somebody help me, before I OD on an LP
Take me to ER ASAP for an IV
Motherfuck JLB, they don't support no hip-hop
They say that's where it lives, the closest they gon' come is Tupac
It's politics, it's all a fix
Set up by these white blue-collared hicks
Just to make a dollar off of black music
With a subliminal ball of tricks
For those who kiss ass and swallow dicks

CHORUS

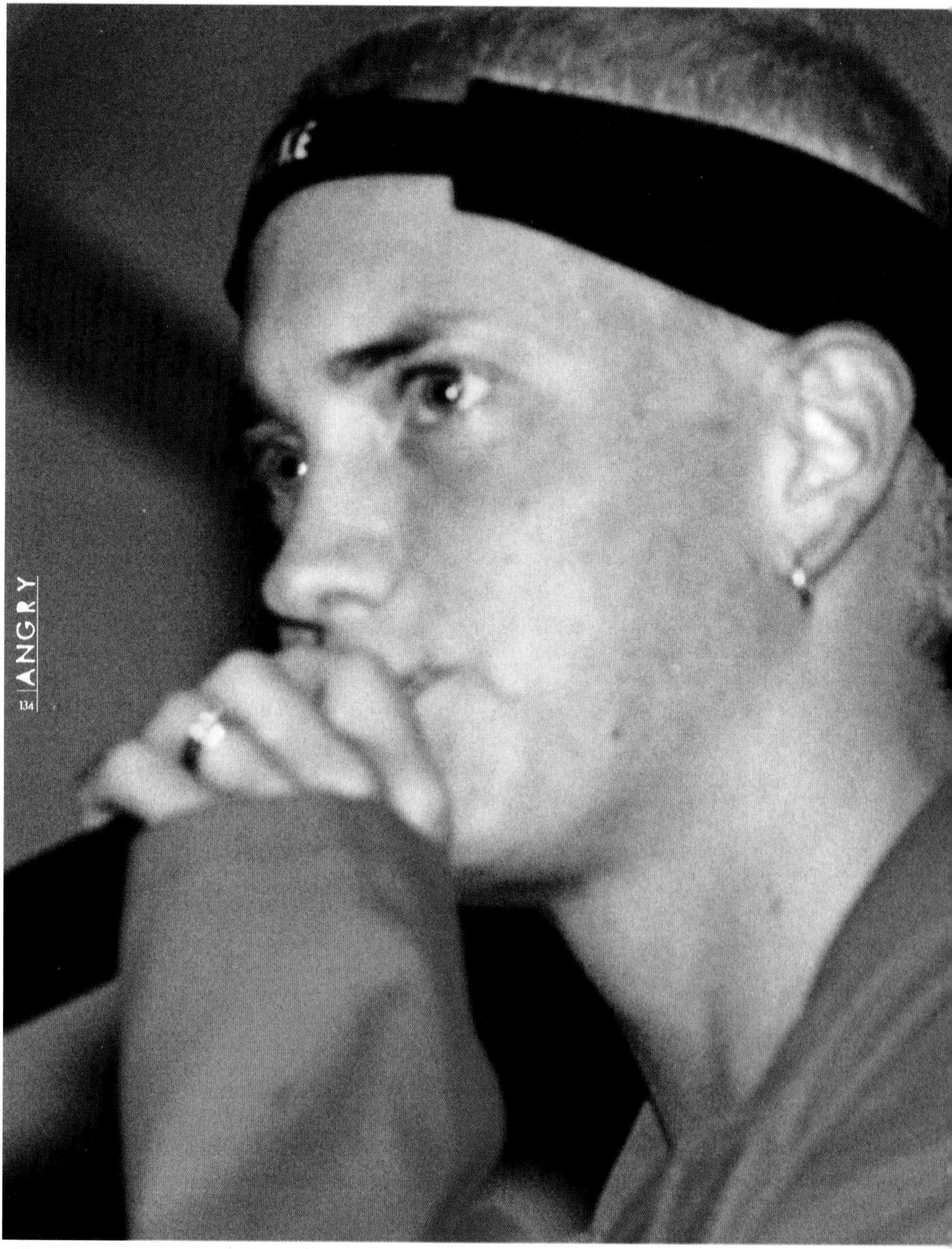

INFINITE

The Hip-Hop Shop was a spot in Detroit where all of the city's illest emcees would meet. It was a regular hangout for me. Back in the Hip-Hop Shop days, there were verses that I would throw out in the shop. I would just use them in there. Once I started getting a rep, I actually used one of those verses for an open mic and people were trippin' on it, so I thought "Fuck it. I gotta finish it." I finished the verses and made them into this song. D-12's Denaun (aka Kon Artis) used to do all my beats and he had the original track. I personally think this was the best song I did on that album. That was '95, '96—the era of just rhyming for the hell of it. People at one point actually said I sounded like Nas, 'cause I used all these big words. This is show-your-skill type shit.

Oh yeah, this is Eminem, baby, back up in that motherfucking ass
One time for your motherfucking mind, we represent the 313
You know what I'm saying? 'Cause they don't know shit about this
For the 9-6

Ayo, my pen and paper cause a chain reaction
Brain relaxin', a zany-actin' maniac
You look insanely wack when just a fraction of my tracks run
My rhyming skills got you climbing hills
I travel through your spine like siren drills
I'm sliming grills of roaches with spray that disinfects
And twistin' necks of rappers so their spinal column disconnects
Put this in your decks and then check the monologue, turn your system up
Twist them up, and indulge in the marijuana smog
This is the season for noise pollution contamination
Examination of more cartoons than animation
My lamination of narration

Hits the snare and bass of a track for wack rapper interrogation
When I declare invasion, there ain't no time to be starin' and gazing
I'll turn the stage to a barren wasteland . . .
I'm Infinite

CHORUS:
YOU HEARD OF HELL, WELL, I WAS SENT FROM IT
I WENT TO IT SERVIN' A SENTENCE FOR MURDERING INSTRUMENTS
NOW I'M TRYING TO REPENT FROM IT
BUT WHEN I HEAR THE BEAT I'M TEMPTED TO MAKE ANOTHER ATTEMPT AT IT . . .
I'M INFINITE

Bust it, I let the beat commence so I can beat the sense of your elite defense
I got some meat to mince
A crew to stomp and then two feet to rinse
I greet the gents and ladies, I spoil loyal fans
I foil plans and leave fluids leaking like oil pans
My coiled hands around this microphone is lethal

One thought in my cerebral is deeper than a Jeep full of people

MC's are feeble, I came to cause some pandemonium
Battle a band of phony MC's and stand a lonely one

Imitator, Intimidator, Stimulator, Simulator of data, Eliminator
There's never been a greater since the burial of Jesus
Fuck around and catch all of the venereal diseases
My thesis will smash a stereo to pieces
My a cappella releases plastic masterpieces through telekinesis
That eases you mentally, gently, sentimentally, instrumentally
With entity, dementedly meant to be Infinite

CHORUS:
YOU HEARD OF HELL, WELL, I WAS SENT FROM IT
I WENT TO IT SERVIN' A SENTENCE FOR MURDERING INSTRUMENTS
NOW I'M TRYING TO REPENT FROM IT
BUT WHEN I HEAR THE BEAT I'M TEMPTED TO MAKE ANOTHER ATTEMPT AT IT . . .
I'M INFINITE

Man, I got evidence I'm never dense and I been clever ever since
My residence was hesitant to do some shit that represents the MO
So I'm assuming all responsibility
'Cause there's a monster will in me that always wants to kill MC's
Mic Nestler, slamming like a wrestler
Here to make a mess of a lyric-smuggling embezzler
No one is specialer, my skill is intergalactical
I get cynical at a fool, then I send a crew back to school
I never packed a tool or acted cool, it wasn't practical
I'd rather let a tactical, tactful, track tickle your fancy
In fact I can't see, or can't imagine
A man who ain't a lover of
beats or a fan of scratchin'
So this is for my family, the kid who had a cammy on my last jam
Plus the man who never had a plan B, be all you can be, 'cause once you make an instant hit I'm tensed
a bit and tempted when I see the sins my friends commit . . .
I'm Infinite

CHORUS:
YOU HEARD OF HELL WELL I WAS SENT FROM IT
I WENT TO IT SERVING A SENTENCE FOR MURDERING INSTRUMENTS
NOW I'M TRYING TO REPENT FROM IT
BUT WHEN I HEAR THE BEAT I'M TEMPTED TO MAKE ANOTHER ATTEMPT AT IT . . .
I'M INFINITE

You heard of hell well I was sent from it
I went to it serving a sentence for murdering instruments
Now I'm trying to repent from it
But when I hear the beat I'm tempted to make another attempt at it . . .
I'm Infinite

FREESTYLE
FROM
TONY TOUCH'S
POWER
CYPHA 3

If I'm elected for ten terms
I'm renewing the staff after the inaugural
And hiring all girls as interns
If I don't like you, I'll snatch you outta your mic booth
While you're rappin' and pull you right through the window and fight you
I'll take you straight to the pavement
Uppercut you, and scrape your face wit' a bracelet like a razor just shaved it
Three drinks and I'm ready to flash
Runnin' onstage in a G-string, wit' a bee sting on my ass (Look!)
It's probably y'all 'cause I ain't awkward at all
I just like to walk through the mall, stop, and talk to the wall
And have a relapse after I just fought through withdrawal
(Hop in the car, little girl, I just bought you a doll)

The Bad and Evil movement is comin'
Plus the music is pumpin' like a pill freak wit' a tube in his stomach

I write a rhyme a day so it's no wonder how come your whole album
Is soundin' like a bunch of shit that I would say
Whether it's one verse or one letter
I'll probably be the cleverest one that never gets spun, ever
It's Slim Shady and Tony Touch, it's only us
The rest of y'all are just stuck in the middle wit' Monie Love

Some people say I'm strange, I tell them ain't shit change
I'm still the same lame asshole with a different name
Who came late to the last show with a different dame
Brain ate from the last "O" that I sniffed of caine
You know you're spaced the fuck out like George Lucas when your puke is
turnin' to yellowish-orange mucus
So when I grab a pencil and squeeze it between fingers
I'm not a rapper, I'm a demon who speaks English

3HREE 6IX 5IVE

Freak genius, too extreme for the weak and squeamish
Burn you alive till you screamin' to be extinguished
'Cause when I drop the science, motherfuckers tell me to stop the violence
Start a fire and block the hydrants
I'm just a mean person, you never seen worse than
So when Slim gets this M-16 burstin'
You gettin' spun backwards like every word of obscene cursin'
On the B-side of my first single with the clean version
Stoppin' your short life while you're still a teen virgin
Unless you get a kidney specialist and a spleen surgeon
In the best hospital possible for emergency surgery
To try to stop the blood from your ruptured sternum internally
I'll take it back before we knew each other's name
Run in a ultrasound and snatch you out your mother's frame
I'll take it further back than that
Back to Lovers' Lane, to the night you were thought of, and
Cock-block your father's game
I plead the fifth like my jaws were muzzled
So suck my dick while I take a shit and do this crossword puzzle
And when I'm down with ten seconds left in the whole bout
I'ma throw a head-butt so hard, I'll knock us both out

Yo, weed lacer, '97 burgundy Blazer
Wanted for burglary, had to ditch the Mercury Tracer
I'm on some loc'd shit
Some fed up wit' the bein' broke shit
I'm not to joke wit'

WEED LACER
(FREESTYLE)

Bitch, I don't sell crack, I smoke it
My brain's dusted; I'm disgusted at all my habits
Too many aspirin tablets, empty medicine cabinets
Losing battles to wack rappers 'cause I'm always too blunted
Walkin' up in the cypher smokin', talkin' 'bout "Who want it?"
Thug and crook; every drug in the book I've done it
My 9's at your brain, is that your chain? Run it
Crews die from an overdosage of excessive flavor
Aggressive nature got me stickin' you for your Progressive pager
Spectacular, crystal-meth manufacturer
Stole your momma's Acura, wrecked it, and sold it back to her
Boostin' Nike jackets, escaped from psychiatrics
Told the nurse to save a bed for me, I might be back, bitch
So barricade your entrance, put up some extra fences
A woman beater, wanted for repeated sex offenses (Ooh)
Chasin' dips—take 'em on long vacation trips
Kidnappin' 'em and trappin' 'em in abusive relationships
Fuck up your face and lips
Slit your stomach and watch your gut split
Gut you wit' that razor that I use to shave my nuts wit' [laughter]
Mama, don't you cry, your son is too far gone
I'm so high, I don't even know what label I'm on
I'm fucked up, I feel just like an overworked plumber
I'm sick of this shit, what's Dr. Kevorkian's phone number?

PILLS
(FREESTYLE)

Performed live at Tramps, New York City, January 7, 1999

Well, I do pop pills

I keep my tube socks filled
And pop the same shit that got Tupac killed
Spit game to these hos
Like a soap opera episode
Then punch a bitch in the nose
Until her whole face explodes
There's three things I hate: girls, women, and bitches
I'm that vicious to talk up and drop-kick midgets
They call me "Boogie Night"
A stalker that walks awkward
Stick figure with a dick bigger than Mark Wahlberg
Coming through the airport sluggish, walking on crutches
And hit a pregnant bitch in the stomach with luggage

It's like a dream, I can't back out, I black out I'm back out, looking for someone "of" to beat the "crap out"

I'm bringing you rap singers
Two middle fingers
Flip you off in French and translate it in English
Then I'm gonna vanish from the face of this planet
And come back speaking so much Spanish that Pun can't even understand it

PHOTO CREDITS

PHOTO CAPTIONS

ii–iii	"The Real Slim Shady" video shoot in Los Angeles.
vi–vii	Backstage at Hammerstein Ballroom, New York. April 15, 1999.
ix–x	Em performing at the Hammerstein Ballroom.
02	Marshall Mathers III at two-and-a-half years old.
05	Em in Amsterdam. November 1999.
13	The Up in Smoke Tour, Meadowbrook Farms, New Hampshire. July 24, 2000.
16	"The Real Slim Shady" video shoot in Los Angeles. Britney Spears, eat your heart out!
17	Pre-show at the Up in Smoke Tour, Meadowbrook Farms.
18–19	In Amsterdam. November 1999.
22–23	A ticket to Eminem's first show at the Hammerstein Ballroom.
24–25	Eminem and the mummy (Rasta style) live on the Vans Warped Tour. June 1999.
41	Eminem outside the house in Dresden, Michigan, where he spent most of his adolescence.
43	DJ Head onstage at the Hammerstein Ballroom.
48–51	High-fives for everyone. Em and Proof live on the Vans Warped Tour. Summer 1999.
52–53	At the hotel during the Up in Smoke Tour in Denver, Colorado. August 19, 2000.
54–55	Dr. Dre at Encore Studios in Los Angeles. February 2000.
59	The real Les Nessman at "The Real Slim Shady" video shoot in Los Angeles.
62–63	During the Up in Smoke Tour in Denver.
64–65	Eminem during the Slim Shady European Tour. Fall 1999.
66	At the Up In Smoke Tour, Meadowbrook Farms.
72–77	Outside of Gilbert's Lodge in St. Claire Shores, Michigan. February 2000.
84–88	A New York City studio shot. April 15, 1999.
90–93	Em strung out on microphones during the Vans Warped Tour. Summer 1999.
94–95	On the Vans Warped Tour. June 1999.
96	Eminem and Paul "Bunyan" Rosenberg back-to-back at the "Way I Am" video shoot at Universal Studios in Los Angeles. June 2000.
104–105	Eminem as Houdini during the video shoot for "Role Model."
106–109	Eminem and his brothers at the video shoot for "The Real Slim Shady."

PHOTO INSERT

LYRIC CREDITS

If I Had . . . : 8 Mile Style/Ensign Music Corporation (BMI)
Brain Damage: 8 Mile Style/Ensign Music Corporation (BMI)
Role Model: 8 Mile Style/Ensign Music Corporation/Ain't Nothing But F****n Music (BMI)
Guilty Conscience: 8 Mile Style/Ensign Music Corporation/Ain't Nothing But F****n Music (BMI)
The Kids: 8 Mile Style/Ensign Music Corporation (BMI)
Marshall Mathers: 8 Mile Style/Ensign Music Corporation (BMI)
Criminal: 8 Mile Style/Ensign Music Corporation (BMI)
As the World Turns: 8 Mile Style/Ensign Music Corporation (BMI)
Kim: 8 Mile Style/Ensign Music Corporation (BMI)
Amityville: 8 Mile Style/Ensign Music Corporation (BMI)
Drug Ballad: 8 Mile Style/Ensign Music Corporation (BMI)
The Way I Am: 8 Mile Style/Ensign Music Corporation (BMI)
Kill You: 8 Mile Style/Ensign Music Corporation/Ain't Nothing But F****n Music (BMI)
Who Knew: 8 Mile Style/Ensign Music Corporation/Ain't Nothing But F****n Music (BMI)
The Real Slim Shady: 8 Mile Style/Ensign Music Corporation/Ain't Nothing But F****n Music (BMI)
I'm Back: 8 Mile Style/Ensign Music Corporation/Ain't Nothing But F****n Music (BMI)
Two Freestyles from the D.J. Stretch Armstrong Presents The Slim Shady LP Snippet Tape: 8 Mile Style (BMI)
Any Man: 8 Mile Style (BMI)
Murder Murder (Remix) : 8 Mile Style (BMI)
Bad Influence: 8 Mile Style (BMI)
Fuck the Planet (freestyle) : 8 Mile Style (BMI)
No One's Iller Than Me: 8 Mile Style (BMI)
Low Down, Dirty: 8 Mile Style (BMI)
Infinite: 8 Mile Style/Ensign Music Corporation (BMI)
Freestyle from Tony Touch's Power Cypha 3: 8 Mile Style (BMI)
3hreeSix5ive: 8 Mile Style (BMI)
Weed Lacer (freestyle) : 8 Mile Style (BMI)
Pills (freestyle) : 8 Mile Style (BMI)

Eminem Management: Paul D. Rosenberg, Esq. for Goliath Artists, Inc.
Eminem Agent: United Talent Agency
Eminem Legal: Cutler & Sedlmayr, LLP
Angry Blonde photo consultant: Stuart Parr for Cousins Entertainment, Inc.
Lyrics compiled and edited by: Paul Rosenberg with assistance from Marc Labelle and Jacob Kallio.
Introduction by: Eminem with Riggs Morales